Collins

CRICKET
QUIZ
BOOK

HarperCollins Publishers
Westerhill Road
Bishopbriggs
Glasgow
G64 2QT

First Edition 2012

Reprint 10 9 8 7 6 5 4 3 2 1 0

© HarperCollins Publishers 2012

ISBN 978-0-00-747995-5

Collins® is a registered trademark of
HarperCollins Publishers Limited

www.collinslanguage.com

A catalogue record for this book is
available from the British Library

Typeset by Davidson Publishing
Solutions, Glasgow

Printed in Great Britain by Clays Ltd,
St Ives plc

Acknowledgements
We would like to thank those authors
and publishers who kindly gave
permission for copyright material
to be used in the Collins Corpus.
We would also like to thank Times
Newspapers Ltd for providing
valuable data.

AUTHOR
Chris Bradshaw

EDITOR
Gerry Breslin
Freddy Chick

FOR THE PUBLISHER
Lucy Cooper
Julianna Dunn
Kerry Ferguson
Elaine Higgleton

Introduction

The fact that cricket exists is probably a lot more important to philosophy than has so far been realised. It must either be the gift of the gods or proof that heavenly ideas lurk within man's soul. Indeed, in *The Hitchhiker's Guide to the Galaxy*, Douglas Adams goes even further by suggesting that the only reason that Planet Earth was created was so that a race of pan-dimensional beings could get on with their game of Brockian Ultra - Cricket in peace.

Whoever was responsible for its invention, they certainly understood that one of the key roles of any sport is to produce statistics and trivia for fans to pore over. Cricket is in a league of its own here. Commentary teams actually need to have a full-time statistician just to keep up with all the facts and figures that are going on in a game. There is even the Duckworth-Lewis method, a statistical formula used to determine the winner of matches!

Besides statistics there are, of course, the great players and teams that have graced cricket over the years; from the larger-than-life W.G. Grace, the unequalled Bradman and the great West Indian or Australian sides, to the talented antics of a Flintoff or an Afridi in recent years.

The end result is that cricket is the perfect sport for a quiz. *Collins Cricket Quiz Book* tests your knowledge of all aspects of the game. County cricket and test internationals, ODI and Twenty20. It's the ideal accompaniment to an afternoon at the cricket, watching it on TV or listening on the radio.

The quizzes

The quizzes are grouped together according to how tricky they are. First come the easy ones, then the medium and finally the difficult quizzes.

Easy

Think of these quizzes batting in the nets. You should be swinging freely and knocking most of them away with ease. There are a few trickier ones thrown in here that some umpires might rate as 'challenging'. This is to build in the frisson of a mental sweat.

Medium

If you're the sort of person that reads Wisden late into the night, then these questions shouldn't pose too much trouble. Otherwise, get ready for a testing mix of quizzes.

Difficult

These are real snorters that will have you fishing for the answer. Anyone who is getting them right deserves respect. Anyone who gets them all right, you should suspect of foul play and ask to see their smartphone's browser history.

The answers

The answers to each quiz are printed at the end of the following quiz. For example, the answers to Quiz 1-Pot Luck appear at the bottom of Quiz 2-The Ashes. The exception to this rule is the last quiz in every level. The answers to these quizzes appear at the end of the very first quiz in the level.

Running a quiz

Collins Cricket Quiz Book is only half-finished. (Wait! Don't demand a refund yet, read on!) People don't go to the theatre to sit and read a script. Likewise, the quizzes in this book need someone to read them out. That's you.

If you're just quizzing your family during a car journey, or your mates of an afternoon, then there's probably no need to put in lots of preparation. If you're planning on using this book to run a more organized and formal quiz, however, there are a few things you need to get right before you start.

- Rehearse: don't just pick this book up and read out the questions cold. Go through all the quizzes you're going to use by yourself beforehand. Note down all the questions (notes look better in a quiz environment than reading from a book) and answers. Although every effort has been made to ensure that all the answers in *Collins Cricket Quiz Book* are correct, despite our best endeavours, mistakes may still appear. If you see an answer you are not sure is right, or if you think there is more than one possible answer, then check.

- Paper and writing implements: do yourself a favour and prepare enough sheets of paper for everyone to write on. The aim of the game here is to stop the mad impulse certain people feel to 'help'. They will spend ten minutes running around looking for 'scrap' paper, probably ripping up your latest novel in the process. The same problem applies to pens. Ideally, have enough for everyone. Remember, though, that over half of them will be lost forever once you've given them out. You can use the 'Keeping Score' pages at the back of the book to record the quiz scores for each team or person.

- Prizes: everyone likes a prize. Since this is a sports quiz book, your audience will probably not understand the concept of a competition without one. No matter how small, it's best to have one on offer.

Good luck! We hope you enjoy *Collins Cricket Quiz Book*.

Contents

Easy Quizzes

Medium Quizzes

Difficult Quizzes

EASY QUIZZES

Quiz 1: Pot Luck

1. Lord's is the home ground of which English county?

2. What colour kit do Australia usually wear in One-Day Internationals?

3. What middle name is shared by England bowlers Tim Bresnan and Steve Finn?

4. Who is England's all-time leading Test wicket-taker?

5. Which broadcaster likes to 'start the car'?

6. With 950 runs, who was England's leading Test run-scorer in 2011?

7. What do the initials MCC stand for?

8. Grace Road is the home ground of which English county?

9. The badges of which two English counties feature three seaxes?

10. Umpires Rob Bailey, Peter Willey, Neil Mallender and George Sharp all played for which county?

11. Lightning is the nickname of which English county side?

12. Who was the oldest member of England's 2010/11 Ashes-winning squad?

13. Which legendary West Indian bowler has the middle names Elconn Lynwall?

14. What is the only South American country that hosts Test cricket?

15. Who was the first Welshman to score 10,000 runs and take 1,000 wickets in first-class cricket?

16. Ian Bell and Jonathan Trott play domestic cricket for which English county?

17. Which cricketer is a team captain on A Question of Sport?

18. Australians call them wrong'uns. What are they known as in England?

19. Matthew Hoggard left Yorkshire to take up the captaincy at which county?
    a) Derbyshire
    b) Leicestershire
    c) Northamptonshire

20. In which Australian city will you find a ground called The WACA?
    a) Adelaide
    b) Brisbane
    c) Perth

Answers to Quiz 33: Pot Luck

1. Jimmy Adams
2. Samit Patel
3. The Frank Worrell Trophy
4. Ajmal Shahzad
5. Chris Broad, Michael Vaughan and Alastair Cook
6. Ravi Bopara
7. Gloucestershire
8. Chris Adams
9. Dermot Reeve
10. Ryan Harris
11. West Indies
12. Bob Willis
13. Colin Miller
14. Yuvraj Singh and Ravi Shastri
15. Andrew Flintoff and Steve Harmison
16. Sri Lanka
17. Yorkshire
18. The Cricketer
19. Shane Warne
20. Birmingham

Quiz 2: The Ashes

EASY

1. Who captained England to victory in the 2010/11 Ashes?

2. Who was on the receiving end of the delivery dubbed 'The Ball of the Century'?

3. Which opener scored a hat trick of centuries during England's 1986/87 triumph?

4. Who were England's two double centurions in the 2010/11 series?

5. Who is the all-time leading wicket-taker in Ashes matches?

6. Who skippered England to victory in the 1970/71 series?

7. How many times were the Aussies on the wrong end of an innings defeat in the 2010/11 series?

8. With 148 scalps, who is England's leading wicket-taker in Ashes matches?

9. Which spinner took 46 wickets for England in the 1956 Ashes series?

10. What did England's sixth, seventh and eighth wicket partnerships do in Sydney in 2010/11 that had never been done in Test cricket before?

11. What was the margin of victory in the first Ashes Test and the Melbourne Centenary Test?

12. Which Yorkshireman compiled England's highest individual score against Australia?

13. Which two players captained England during the famous 1981 Ashes series?

14. Which left-hander scored 732 runs at an average of 81.33 in the 1985 Ashes?

15. Who has captained an Ashes team on the most occasions?

16. How many times did England top 500 in an innings in the 2010/11 series?

17. Who was the England captain during the infamous 'Bodyline' series?

18. Which Aussie took 16 wickets on his Test debut at Lord's in 1972?

19. In what year did the first Ashes Test take place?
     a) 1876
     b) 1877
     c) 1878

20. What was the venue for the first ever Ashes Test?
     a) Lord's
     b) The MCG
     c) The Oval

Answers to Quiz 1: Pot Luck

1. Middlesex
2. Yellow
3. Thomas
4. Ian Botham
5. David Lloyd
6. Ian Bell
7. Marylebone Cricket Club
8. Leicestershire
9. Essex and Middlesex
10. Northamptonshire
11. Lancashire
12. Paul Collingwood
13. Curtly Ambrose
14. Guyana
15. Robert Croft
16. Warwickshire
17. Phil Tufnell
18. Googlies
19. Leicestershire
20. Perth

Quiz 3: Pot Luck

1. Complete the title of the 2005 book: Is it Cowardly to Pray for...?

2. WG Grace played domestic cricket for which English county?

3. Which Lancashire left-arm spinner has taken over 650 first-class wickets but has never played for England?

4. Which England wicket-keeper made a century on his Test debut at Lord's in 2007?

5. Who were the original sponsors of England's Sunday League?

6. Which county's ground has a tree on the field of play?

7. The Wall is the nickname of which Indian batsman?

8. Which ground hosted its first Test match when England faced Sri Lanka in 2011?

9. Which umpire has officiated in both football and cricket World Cup matches?

10. What is the name of Cambridge University's home ground?

11. Who captained England on the 2002/03 Ashes tour to Australia?

12. Which England bowler took four wickets in an over in a Test match against the West Indies at Headingley in 2000?

13. Which former Somerset and England spinner is the cricket correspondent for The Observer?

14. Which cricketer won the Beard of the Year Award in 2004 and 2005?

15. Who were the 2010 County Champions?

16. Who made 112 and 83 on his Test debut against New Zealand at Lord's in 2004?

17. Who was the first Bangladeshi cricketer to be named one of Wisden's Five Cricketers of the Year?

18. Stuart Broad started his county career with which side?

19. Which country will host the 2019 Cricket World Cup?
    a) England
    b) India
    c) South Africa

20. Who is the only player to score more than ten Test match double hundreds?
    a) Don Bradman
    b) Brian Lara
    c) Sachin Tendulkar

Answers to Quiz 2: The Ashes

1. Andrew Strauss
2. Mike Gatting
3. Chris Broad
4. Alastair Cook and Kevin Pietersen
5. Shane Warne
6. Raymond Illingworth
7. Three
8. Ian Botham
9. Jim Laker
10. They all put on 100 runs or more
11. Australia won by 45 runs in both
12. Len Hutton
13. Ian Botham and Mike Brearley
14. David Gower
15. Allan Border
16. Five
17. Douglas Jardine
18. Bob Massie
19. 1877
20. The MCG

Quiz 4: England

1. Who captained England on their 2010 tour of Bangladesh?

2. Can you name the three England batsmen who scored Test double centuries in the 2011 series against India?

3. Who was the first Englishman to score 8,000 Test match runs?

4. Which pair set the record for the highest eighth-wicket partnership in Test history against Pakistan in 2010?

5. Who succeeded Michael Vaughan as captain of England's Test team?

6. Who went 54 innings at the start of his Test career without being dismissed for a duck?

7. Which England batsman scored centuries in three successive Test innings in 2009?

8. Who holds the record for the most Test wickets in a calendar year by an England bowler?

9. Spinners Monty Panesar and Graeme Swann started their careers with which county?

10. Who scored centuries in three consecutive Tests against the great West Indian side in 1984 but was on the losing side in every match?

11. Who scored his maiden Test century against Pakistan at Trent Bridge in 2010?

12. Alastair Cook scored a century on his Test debut in 2006. Who were England's opponents?

13. Who took over as England's bowling coach in April 2010?

14. Who hit the winning runs in England's 2010 World T20 triumph?

15. Which five England players were named in the 2011 ICC World Test team?

16. Who is the only England player to appear in three World Cup finals?

17. Who was the man of the match in the 2010 World Twenty20 final?

18. Who holds the record for the highest Test innings by an England wicket-keeper?

19. In 1999, England dropped to the bottom of the world Test rankings after a home series defeat to which country?
    a) India
    b) New Zealand
    c) Zimbabwe

20. Which bowler took the most Test wickets?
    a) Matthew Hoggard
    b) Andrew Caddick
    c) Darren Gough

Answers to Quiz 3: Pot Luck

1. Rain
2. Gloucestershire
3. Gary Keedy
4. Matt Prior
5. John Player
6. Kent
7. Rahul Dravid
8. Rose Bowl, Southampton
9. Steve Bucknor
10. Fenners
11. Nasser Hussain
12. Andrew Caddick
13. Vic Marks
14. Andrew Flintoff
15. Nottinghamshire
16. Andrew Strauss
17. Tamim Iqbal
18. Leicestershire
19. England
20. Don Bradman

Quiz 5: Pot Luck

1. How many ways can a batsman be dismissed?

2. What method is used to decide results in rain-affected games?

3. What is signified if an umpire raises one arm above his head?

4. With 563 wickets, who is the leading fast bowler in Test cricket history?

5. A rose topped by a crown features on the badges of which two English counties?

6. The Outlaws is the nickname of which county side?

7. Which Australian quickie's surname is the same as a type of champagne?

8. In a cricket scorebook, what does + represent?

9. Andrew Flintoff advised which West Indian bowler to 'mind the windows' during the 2004 Lord's Test?

10. Who is England's leading run-scorer in Test cricket?

11. What flower is on the badge of Lancashire?

12. Dominic Cork played for which three English counties?

13. At which Test ground will you find the Western Terrace?

14. Who in world cricket has won the most Test match caps?

15. Who captained England on the 2006/07 Ashes tour to Australia?

16. Which England captain was nicknamed 'The Ayatollah' after sporting a particularly impressive beard?

17. New Road is the home ground of which English county?

18. Who holds the record for the most runs for England in a Test series since the war?

19. What is the narrowest margin of victory in the history of Test cricket?
    a) 1 run
    b) 2 runs
    c) 3 runs

20. Who did Michael Vaughan succeed as captain of the England Test team?
    a) Michael Atherton
    b) Nasser Hussain
    c) Alec Stewart

Answers to Quiz 4: England

1. Alastair Cook
2. Kevin Pietersen, Ian Bell and Alastair Cook
3. Geoffrey Boycott
4. Jonathan Trott and Stuart Broad
5. Kevin Pietersen
6. James Anderson
7. Ravi Bopara
8. Andrew Flintoff with 68 in 2005
9. Northamptonshire
10. Allan Lamb
11. Eoin Morgan
12. India
13. David Saker
14. Paul Collingwood
15. Alastair Cook, Jonathan Trott, Stuart Broad, Graeme Swann and James Anderson
16. Graham Gooch
17. Craig Kieswetter
18. Alec Stewart
19. New Zealand
20. Matthew Hoggard

Quiz 6: Cricket World Cup

1. What was the venue for the first three World Cup finals?

2. Who did India beat in the 2011 final?

3. Who were the winners of the first two World Cups?

4. Which Australian scored an unbeaten 140 from just 121 balls in the 2003 final?

5. Which Pakistani spinner was the joint leading wicket-taker at the 2011 World Cup?

6. Who is the only player to score more than 2000 runs in World Cup games?

7. Australia beat which country in the 2007 final?

8. Which country has reached the World Cup semifinal six times but never played in the final?

9. Who captained the winning Indian team in 1983?

10. Who is the only wicket-keeper to captain a side to victory in a World Cup final?

11. Which four non-Test-playing nations took part in the 2011 World Cup?

12. Who thrashed England by 10 wickets in the 2011 quarter final?

13. Which umpire stood in his fifth World Cup final in 2007?

14. Who is the only man to play in World Cup matches at both football and cricket?

15. Which team surprisingly reached the semifinal in 2003 after beating Sri Lanka and Zimbabwe?

16. Who beat England in the 1992 final?

17. Which two countries will host the 2015 World Cup?

18. Which South African hit six sixes in an over against the Netherlands in 2007?

19. Ireland shocked which country in the 2007 competition?
    a) India
    b) New Zealand
    c) Pakistan

20. How many World Cup finals have England lost?
    a) 2
    b) 3
    c) 4

Answers to Quiz 5: Pot Luck

1. Ten
2. The Duckworth-Lewis method
3. A bye
4. Glenn McGrath
5. Derbyshire and Hampshire
6. Nottinghamshire
7. Doug Bollinger
8. A wide
9. Tino Best
10. Graham Gooch

11. Red rose
12. Derbyshire, Lancashire and Hampshire
13. Headingley
14. Sachin Tendulkar
15. Andrew Flintoff
16. Mike Brearley
17. Worcestershire
18. Alastair Cook
19. 1 run
20. Nasser Hussain

Quiz 7: Pot Luck

EASY

1. Who did Andy Flower succeed as coach of the England team?

2. Which five nations hosted a World Cup match in 1999?

3. Which team suffered an innings defeat against England in Cardiff in 2011 despite scoring 400 in their first innings?

4. Which Lancashire all-rounder was named one of Wisden's Five Cricketers of the Year in 2012?

5. What does it mean if an umpire taps on his shoulder with one hand?

6. In Test matches, a new ball is available to the fielding side after how many overs?

7. Which county's one-day team is nicknamed The Falcons?

8. Which Hampshire batsman has the same name as a former captain of the West Indies?

9. Which Australian was appointed coach of Yorkshire for the 2012 season?

10. BBC cricket correspondent Jonathan Agnew played for which English county?

11. Which country scored a mammoth 952-6 in a Test match in 1997?

12. How many runs did Don Bradman score in his final Test innings?

13. Who was England's leading Test wicket-taker in 2011?

14. In a cricket scorebook, what is signified by a circle?

15. Michael Atherton writes for which newspaper?

16. Which coach died shortly after his team were eliminated from the 2007 World Cup?

17. Who was the BBC's first cricket correspondent?

18. Who was appointed England's spin bowling coach in 2009?

19. Which Test ground is overlooked by Lumley Castle?
    a) The Riverside
    b) The Rose Bowl
    c) Swalec Stadium

20. What fruit appears on the badge of Worcestershire CCC?
    a) apple
    b) pear
    c) plum

Answers to Quiz 6: Cricket World Cup

1. Lord's
2. Sri Lanka
3. West Indies
4. Ricky Ponting
5. Shahid Afridi
6. Sachin Tendulkar
7. Sri Lanka
8. New Zealand
9. Kapil Dev
10. MS Dhoni
11. Canada, Ireland, Kenya and the Netherlands
12. Sri Lanka
13. Steve Bucknor
14. Sir Viv Richards
15. Kenya
16. Pakistan
17. Australia and New Zealand
18. Herschelle Gibbs
19. Pakistan
20. 3

Quiz 8: The Ashes 2009

1. What was the score in the series?

2. Which city hosted the first Test?

3. Which last wicket pair saved the day for England in the opening match?

4. Who became Australia's leading Test run-scorer during the series?

5. There was another crucial last-wicket stand in the second Test. Which pair put on 47 in England's first innings?

6. Which two English batsmen scored centuries during the series?

7. Who batted at number three for England in the first four matches?

8. Who was England's leading wicket-taker in the series?

9. Two Australians scored two centuries during the 2009 Ashes. Michael Clarke was one, who was the other?

10. Which Australian spinner dislocated his finger while attempting to catch Andrew Strauss at Lord's?

11. England were walloped by an innings and 80 runs at which ground?

12. Which Australian bowler claimed his 100th Test wicket when dismissing Alastair Cook at Lord's?

13. How many of England's 2005 Ashes-winning squad were also involved in the 2009 triumph?

14. Who took four wickets in five overs to swing the final Test in England's direction?

15. Which Australian seamer was the leading wicket-taker in the series?

EASY

16. Who ran out Ricky Ponting by millimetres in the second innings of the last Test?

17. Which Australian batsman notched up three half-centuries in five innings but never scored more than 62?

18. Who was the winner of the Player of the Series award?

19. Who took the final wicket that clinched the series for England?
    a) Stuart Broad
    b) Andrew Flintoff
    c) Graeme Swann

20. Which batsman was dismissed?
    a) Michael Clarke
    b) Michael Hussey
    c) Brad Haddin

Answers to Quiz 7: Pot Luck

1. Peter Moores
2. England, Scotland, Ireland, Wales and the Netherlands
3. Sri Lanka
4. Glen Chapple
5. The batsmen are one short
6. 80
7. Derbyshire
8. Jimmy Adams
9. Jason Gillespie
10. Leicestershire
11. Sri Lanka
12. None
13. James Anderson
14. A no ball
15. The Times
16. Bob Woolmer
17. Brian Johnston
18. Mushtaq Ahmed
19. Riverside
20. Pear

Quiz 9: Pot Luck

1. In what country do teams compete for the Irani Trophy?

2. If the ball hits an unworn helmet, the batting side is awarded how many runs?

3. Which South African captain was banned for life in 2000 after admitting taking bribes for fixing matches?

4. Which bowler holds the record for the most Test wickets in a calendar year?

5. Who is the youngest England batsman to reach 6,000 Test runs?

6. Which two Australia left-arm seamers opened the bowling in a Test against the West Indies in 2009?

7. Which England batsman was out reverse sweeping in the final of the 1987 World Cup?

8. The City End and the Pavilion End are the rather prosaic names of the ends at which English Test venue?

9. Who is Derbyshire's all-time leading first-class run-scorer?

10. Who was England's bowling coach during the 2005 Ashes series?

11. Which former England captain was part of the BBC's reporting team for the 2012 Masters golf tournament?

12. Players from which team were attacked on their team bus by terrorists in Lahore in 2009?

13. In 2003, who became the first quickie to be recorded bowling at over 100mph in a match?

14. Which England batsman was on the receiving end of the history-making delivery?

15. Which country played their first Test match in 1992?

16. Which England international was surprisingly released by his county just weeks into the 2012 season?

17. Which two sides were involved in the first tied Test match?

18. Who took 64 Test wickets for England in 2010, the most in the world that year?

19. England lost their final five wickets in the Abu Dhabi Test against Pakistan in 2012 in how many balls?
    a) 11
    b) 17
    c) 21

20. Who was the first bowler to take 700 Test wickets?
    a) Anil Kumble
    b) Muttiah Muralitharan
    c) Shane Warne

Answers to Quiz 8: The Ashes 2009

1. England won 2-1
2. Cardiff
3. Monty Panesar and James Anderson
4. Ricky Ponting
5. James Anderson and Graham Onions
6. Andrew Strauss and Jonathan Trott
7. Ravi Bopara
8. Stuart Broad
9. Marcus North
10. Nathan Hauritz
11. Headingley
12. Mitchell Johnson
13. Six
14. Stuart Broad
15. Ben Hilfenhaus
16. Andrew Flintoff
17. Shane Watson
18. Andrew Strauss
19. Graeme Swann
20. Michael Hussey

Quiz 10: County Cricket

1. Which side won the 2011 County Championship?

2. How many points are awarded for a County Championship win?

3. Who were runners-up in both the Clydesdale Bank 40 and Friends Provident T20 competitions in 2011?

4. Which county won the Championship three times in the 2000s?

5. Kevin Pietersen started his English career with which county?

6. Which drinks company was the original sponsor of the County Championship?

7. Which county were dismissed for just 14 by Essex in a Championship game in 1983?

8. Needing a win to claim the title, which team could only manage a draw against Hampshire in the final game of the 2011 County Championship?

9. The martlet appears on the badge of which county?

10. Prior to Durham, what county was admitted to the Championship most recently?

11. Which New Zealander was Warwickshire's overseas pro for the 2012 county season?

12. Which left-hander was the leading run-scorer in the 2011 County Championship?

13. Which county won seven consecutive titles in the 1950s?

14. How many teams are relegated from Division One of the County Championship each season?

15. Simon Brown is the all-time leading wicket-taker for which county?

16. Which side won only one game in the County Championship from 1935 to 1946?

17. Which county won the title for the first time in their history in 2008?

18. Three counties have never won the Championship. Name them.

19. Which county has won the County Championship the most times?
    a) Surrey
    b) Warwickshire
    c) Yorkshire

20. Which county has finished bottom of the County Championship the most times?
    a) Derbyshire
    b) Glamorgan
    c) Northamptonshire

Answers to Quiz 9: Pot Luck

1. India
2. Five
3. Hansie Cronje
4. Shane Warne
5. Alastair Cook
6. Mitchell Johnson and Doug Bollinger
7. Mike Gatting
8. Edgbaston
9. Kim Barnett
10. Troy Cooley
11. Michael Vaughan
12. Sri Lanka
13. Shoaib Akhtar
14. Nick Knight
15. Zimbabwe
16. Ajmal Shahzad
17. Australia and West Indies
18. Graeme Swann
19. 11
20. Shane Warne

Quiz 11: Pot Luck

EASY

1. Whose aluminium bat caused controversy in a Test against England in 1979?

2. What do Australians call extras?

3. Who are the two cricketers to have won Strictly Come Dancing?

4. Dragons appear on the badges of which two English counties?

5. Which big-hitting Yorkshireman was named The Cricket Writers' Club Young Cricketer of the Year in 2011?

6. Brian Lara recorded his record-breaking score of 501 not out against which county?

7. Which former England batsman was bowling when Lara broke the record?

8. The Eric Hollies stand is in which English ground?

9. There have been only two tied matches in the history of Test cricket. Which country was involved in both of them?

10. Umpire Nigel Llong played first-class cricket for which county?

11. Who is the only fielder to have taken 100 ODI catches for England?

12. What animal appears on the Warwickshire CCC badge?

13. What end is opposite the Pavilion End at Lord's?

14. England's highest ODI score of 391 for 4 was compiled against which country?

15. Which Australian media mogul was the founder of World Series Cricket?

16. Who was the first England batsman to score 1,000 international Twenty20 runs?

17. Which England player suffered from a bout of suspected dengue fever while playing in the 2012 IPL?

18. Yasir Arafat plays international cricket for which country?

19. Who has played the most ODIs?
    a) Sanath Jayasuriya
    b) Ricky Ponting
    c) Sachin Tendulkar

20. Which cricketer has won I'm A Celebrity...Get Me Out of Here?
    a) Andrew Flintoff
    b) Darren Gough
    c) Phil Tufnell

Answers to Quiz 10: County Cricket

1. Lancashire	12. Marcus Trescothick
2. 16	13. Surrey
3. Somerset	14. Two
4. Sussex	15. Durham
5. Nottinghamshire	16. Northamptonshire
6. Schweppes	17. Durham
7. Surrey	18. Gloucestershire, Northamptonshire and Somerset
8. Warwickshire	
9. Sussex	19. Yorkshire
10. Glamorgan	20. Derbyshire
11. Jeetan Patel	

Quiz 12: Ashes 2010-11

1. What was the score in the series?

2. Which Australian took a hat trick in the opening Test?

3. Who was England's leading run-scorer in the series?

4. Which player was fined after being caught speeding in a Lamborghini during the series?

5. England declared their second innings in Brisbane on what mammoth score?

6. How many centuries did Alastair Cook compile during the five matches?

7. Who captained Australia in the fifth Test in the absence of the injured Ricky Ponting?

8. Which Australian passed 50 four times but couldn't convert those good starts into three figures?

9. Who were England's three specialist seam bowlers in the final two matches?

10. Which part-time bowler dismissed Michael Clarke with the last ball of the fourth day in Adelaide?

11. Which bowler briefly returned to England between games to be at the birth of his second daughter?

12. Who took 15 wickets for England in the first three matches but was dropped for the final two games?

13. True or false – Paul Collingwood took more catches in the series than Aussie wicket-keeper Brad Haddin?

14. Who was England's leading wicket-taker in the 2010/11 Ashes?

15. Who took the wicket that claimed series victory for England?

16. Who was the only member of England's top seven not to score a century?

17. England dismissed Australia for their lowest-ever score in an Ashes Test in Melbourne. How many did Australia make?

18. Michael Hussey was one of only two Australians to score a century in the series. Who was the other?

19. Which England bowler sent down exactly 1,000 dot balls during the series?
    a) James Anderson
    b) Stuart Broad
    c) Graeme Swann

20. England's players celebrated the series win by performing what sort of dance?
    a) The Flymo
    b) The Sprinkler
    c) The Watering Can

Answers to Quiz 11: Pot Luck

1. Dennis Lillee
2. Sundries
3. Darren Gough and Mark Ramprakash
4. Durham and Somerset
5. Jonny Bairstow
6. Durham
7. John Morris
8. Edgbaston
9. Australia
10. Kent
11. Paul Collingwood
12. Bear
13. The Nursery End
14. Bangladesh
15. Kerry Packer
16. Kevin Pietersen
17. Luke Wright
18. Pakistan
19. Sachin Tendulkar
20. Phil Tufnell

Quiz 13: Pot Luck

EASY

1. England's fastest ever One-Day International hundred was scored by which batsman?

2. What do Australians call groundsmen?

3. The Currie Cup was the original name of the domestic competition in which country?

4. Chef is the nickname of which current England player?

5. Who holds the record for the most dismissals by an England wicket-keeper in ODIs?

6. Coloured clothing was worn at the Cricket World Cup for the first time in which year?

7. Royals is the nickname of the which two county one-day sides?

8. Which cricketer presented ITV cooking show Britain's Best Dish?

9. How many wickets did Bob Willis take in the second innings of the 1981 Ashes Test at Headingley?

10. Pace bowler Jack Brooks plays for which English county?

11. Which country made its Test debut in 1952?

12. Who was Shane Warne talking to when he said, 'You got an MBE, right? For scoring seven at The Oval? That's embarrassing'?

13. Which Australian wicket-keeper has the same name as a former QPR, Manchester City and England footballer?

14. Prior to Michael Vaughan in 2005, who was the last England captain to win the Ashes on home soil?

15. What was the score in the 2006/07 Ashes series?

16. Which three Australians retired from Test cricket after the final Test of that series?

17. Former England captain Nasser Hussain played for which county?

18. At which English ground will you find the Alec Stewart Gate?

19. Ricky Ponting plays domestic cricket in Australia for which state?
    a) New South Wales
    b) Tasmania
    c) Victoria

20. Graeme Hick scored an unbeaten 405 in 1988 against which county?
    a) Somerset
    b) Surrey
    c) Sussex

Answers to Quiz 12: Ashes 2010-11

1. England won 3-1
2. Peter Siddle
3. Alastair Cook
4. Kevin Pietersen
5. 517 for 1
6. Three
7. Michael Clarke
8. Shane Watson
9. James Anderson, Chris Tremlett and Tim Bresnan
10. Kevin Pietersen
11. James Anderson
12. Steven Finn
13. True
14. James Anderson
15. Chris Tremlett
16. Paul Collingwood
17. 98 all out
18. Brad Haddin
19. Graeme Swann
20. The Sprinkler

Quiz 14: Australia

EASY

1. What is the name of the cap worn by members of the Australian Test team?

2. Who is Australia's all-time leading Test run-scorer?

3. In which city will you find the Gabba?

4. Which Australian skipper scored 2,201 runs and took 248 wickets in 63 Test matches?

5. Who holds the record for the most Test match ducks by an Australian batsman?

6. Mr Cricket is the nickname of which prolific batsman?

7. Who are the four Australians to have taken 300 Test wickets?

8. Steve Waugh had spells at Kent and what other English county?

9. Which Australian scored a century from just 69 balls in a Test match against India in 2011/12?

10. What middle name is shared by both Shane Warne and Dennis Lillee?

11. Which rotund batsman set the record for the most cans of beer drunk on a flight from Sydney to London?

12. What was Donald Bradman's final Test batting average?

13. In what year did Australia win their first Cricket World Cup?

14. Who was the Aussie captain on their ill-fated tour of England in 1981?

15. What number is considered unlucky by Australian batsmen?

16. Which fearsome fast bowler said, 'I like to see blood on the pitch'?

Answers – page 31

17. Which Aussie holds the record for the most runs in Test matches without ever making a century?

18. Who holds the record for the highest innings by an Australian in a Test match?

19. Which wicket-keeper has the most Test match dismissals for Australia?
    a) Adam Gilchrist
    b) Ian Healy
    c) Rod Marsh

20. Who has captained Australia in the most Test matches?
    a) Allan Border
    b) Rick Ponting
    c) Steve Waugh

Answers to Quiz 13: Pot Luck

1. Kevin Pietersen
2. Curators
3. South Africa
4. Alastair Cook
5. Alec Stewart
6. 1992
7. Hampshire and Worcestershire
8. Mark Nicholas
9. 8
10. Northamptonshire
11. Pakistan
12. Paul Collingwood
13. Rodney Marsh
14. David Gower in 1985
15. Australia 5-0 England
16. Shane Warne, Glenn McGrath and Justin Langer
17. Essex
18. The Oval
19. Tasmania
20. Somerset

Quiz 15: Pot Luck

EASY

1. Which Australian scored an unbeaten 329 against India in 2011?

2. A stag appears on the badge of which county side?

3. What is the name of Oxford University's home ground?

4. Which former Test cricketer is the leader of the Pakistan Tehreek-e-Insaf political party?

5. Who was appointed captain of England's Twenty20 team in May 2011?

6. The Panthers is the nickname of which English county's one-day side?

7. Kevin Pietersen has played for which three English counties?

8. Which England all-rounder's surname is also name of an Australian Rules Football team?

9. John Walter are the middle names of which former England bowler-turned-commentator?

10. Which bowler is nicknamed 'The Rug' in honour of his hair transplant?

11. Who said he would make the West Indies 'grovel' before the 1976 Test series?

12. What do the initials ICC stand for?

13. Which Warwickshire all-rounder took a world record-tying 7 catches in a 2011 county game?

14. Tugga is the nickname of which Australian Test legend?

15. Which current Football League venue has also hosted a Test match?

16. Peter Moores has coached which two sides to the County Championship title?

17. Who coined the phrase 'corridor of uncertainty'?

18. If a bowler has bagged a 'Michelle', how many wickets has he taken?

19. How many were England dismissed for in the second Test against Pakistan in 2012?
    a) 62
    b) 72
    c) 82

20. Who is the second leading wicket-taker in the history of Test cricket?
    a) Dennis Lillee
    b) Glenn McGrath
    c) Shane Warne

Answers to Quiz 14: Australia

1. The Baggy Green
2. Ricky Ponting
3. Brisbane
4. Richie Benaud
5. Glenn McGrath
6. Michael Hussey
7. Shane Warne, Glenn McGrath, Dennis Lillee and Brett Lee
8. Somerset
9. David Warner
10. Keith
11. David Boon
12. 99.94
13. 1987
14. Kim Hughes
15. 87
16. Jeff Thomson
17. Shane Warne
18. Matthew Hayden with 380
19. Adam Gilchrist
20. Allan Border

Quiz 16: West Indies

1. Which West Indian was the first man to take 500 Test wickets?

2. The fastest century in Test cricket history was scored by which West Indian batsman?

3. Who took over as captain of the West Indies Test team in November 2010?

4. West Indies played a Test match in 2011 where the scores finished level. Who were they playing?

5. Who holds the record for the most Test appearances by a West Indian player?

6. Dwayne Bravo, Ravi Rampaul and Adrian Barath are from which Caribbean island?

7. Sabina Park is in which Caribbean country?

8. Which West Indian scored the first international T20 century?

9. In which two years did the West Indies win the Cricket World Cup?

10. Who smashed a fifty from just 23 balls against the Netherlands in the 2011 Cricket World Cup?

11. Which fast bowler took a tournament best 6 for 27 in the same game?

12. Which all-rounder dismissed Kevin Pietersen hit wicket in a Test match in 2007 and acted as an emergency wicket-keeper in the same game?

13. Who holds the record for the most Test centuries by a West Indian batsman?

14. Which West Indian has been dismissed for a duck the most often in One-Day Internationals?

15. Who is the West Indies' top-scoring wicket-keeper in Test matches?

16. Which fast bowler's mother would ring a bell every time her son took a wicket?

17. Whispering Death was the nickname of which legendary fast bowler?

18. Who holds the record for the highest Test innings by a West Indian in England?

19. England were dismissed for what total against the West Indies in a Test in 2009?
    a) 46
    c) 51
    c) 56

20. Who has captained the West Indies in the most Test matches?
    a) Brian Lara
    b) Clive Lloyd
    c) Viv Richards

Answers to Quiz 15: Pot Luck

1. Michael Clarke
2. Nottinghamshire
3. The Parks
4. Imran Khan
5. Stuart Broad
6. Middlesex
7. Nottinghamshire, Hampshire, Surrey
8. Collingwood
9. Paul Allott
10. Doug Bollinger
11. Tony Greig
12. International Cricket Council
13. Rikki Clarke
14. Steve Waugh
15. Sheffield United's Bramall Lane
16. Sussex and Lancashire
17. Geoffrey Boycott
18. Five
19. 72
20. Shane Warne

Quiz 17: Pot Luck

EASY

1. Who was the first batsman to score a double century in a One-Day International?

2. Who are the four West Indians to have taken 300 Test wickets?

3. Who holds the record for taking the most Test wickets at Lord's?

4. Prior to Andrew Strauss, who was the last England captain to win the Ashes Down Under?

5. In a cricket scorebook, what is represented by an upside-down triangle?

6. Who scored an unbeaten 153 to steer the West Indies to an unlikely one-wicket winner over Australia in Bridgetown in 1999?

7. Which county's one-day side were formerly known as the Sabres?

8. Soul Limbo, the theme to Test Match Special, was recorded by which group?

9. Karl Krikken was the long-time wicket-keeper for which English county?

10. What nationality is umpire Asad Rauf?

11. At which Test venue will you find the Kirkstall Lane End?

12. Which England bowler added the middle name Dylan, as a tribute to his musical hero Bob Dylan?

13. Which England player collected his 300th first-class wicket in Durham's 2012 game against Middlesex?

14. Who was stripped of the England captaincy for taking part in World Series Cricket?

15. Which insurance firm has sponsored the County Championship since 2006?

16. Who scored an unbeaten 173 to steer England to an unlikely Ashes win over Australia at Leeds in 2001?

17. Who, in 2011, became the first team to win eight consecutive T20 internationals?

18. Which county were runners-up in the first two CB 40 finals?

19. What is the lowest total a team has been dismissed for in a Test match?
    a) 26
    b) 36
    c) 46

20. Which country compiled that low total?
    a) Bangladesh
    b) England
    c) New Zealand

Answers to Quiz 16: West Indies

1. Courtney Walsh
2. Viv Richards
3. Darren Sammy
4. India
5. Shivnarine Chanderpaul
6. Trinidad
7. Jamaica
8. Chris Gayle
9. 1975 and 1979
10. Kieron Polland
11. Kemar Roach
12. Dwayne Bravo
13. Brian Lara
14. Chris Gayle
15. Jeffrey Dujon
16. Curtly Ambrose
17. Michael Holding
18. Viv Richards
19. 51
20. Clive Lloyd

Quiz 18: India

1. In what decade did India play their first Test match?

2. Who are the two Indians to have taken more than 400 Test wickets?

3. Which Indian was the first man to score 10,000 Test runs?

4. Who scored 219 in a One-Day International against the West Indies in 2011?

5. Of Indian bowlers who have taken at least 50 Test wickets, which spinner has the best bowling average?

6. Sachin Tendulkar scored his 100th international century in a One-Day International in 2012 against which country?

7. Which leg spinner took 16 wickets on his Test debut against the West Indies in 1988?

8. Which Indian spin bowler scored his maiden Test century in his 121st Test innings against New Zealand in 2010?

9. Which Indian left-arm seamer is the only man to take a hat trick in the opening over of a Test match?

10. Which Indian off spinner took 6 for 47 on his Test debut against the West Indies in Delhi in 2011?

11. Which big-hitting batsman has compiled the three highest Test scores for India?

12. Which New Zealander was the first overseas coach of India?

13. Who did MS Dhoni succeed as captain of India's Test team?

14. Who has captained India in the most Test matches?

15. Who was appointed Indian coach in April 2011?

16. Which former Indian captain was given a life ban after an investigation into match fixing?

17. Very Very Special is the nickname of which stylish Indian batsman?

18. Who was Man of the Match in the 2011 World Cup final?

19. Which Indian has been dismissed for a duck the most times in Test matches?
    a) Zaheer Khan
    b) Anil Kumble
    c) Sachin Tendulkar

20. Who scored India's first T20 century against South Africa in 2010?
    a) Virender Sehwag
    b) Yuvraj Singh
    c) Suresh Raina

Answers to Quiz 17: Pot Luck

1. Sachin Tendulkar
2. Courtney Walsh, Curtly Ambrose, Malcolm Marshall and Lance Gibbs
3. Ian Botham
4. Mike Gatting
5. Leg byes
6. Brian Lara
7. Somerset
8. Booker T and the MGs
9. Derbyshire
10. Pakistani
11. Headingley
12. Bob Willis
13. Graham Onions
14. Tony Greig
15. LV
16. Mark Butcher
17. England
18. Somerset
19. 26
20. New Zealand

Quiz 19: Pot Luck

EASY

1. Which country won the 1996 Cricket World Cup?

2. Who were the third country to play Test cricket after England and Australia?

3. The Australian team dubbed 'The Invincibles' were unbeaten in 31 matches in England in what year?

4. Who scored 374 for Sri Lanka against South Africa in 2006?

5. Which Texan billionaire bankrolled a T20 series in the Caribbean before being found guilty of bank fraud?

6. Which flamboyant umpire is noted for his crooked finger?

7. Who are the only two bowlers to take nine wickets in a Test innings twice?

8. Which country, in 2006, became the first to forfeit a Test match?

9. The Slinger is the nickname of which international bowler?

10. Who is Pakistan's most capped Test player?

11. Which Indian spinner was smashed for 170 in 38 wicketless overs against England at The Oval in 2011?

12. Before becoming the Lions, what was the nickname of Surrey's one-day team?

13. Who scored an unbeaten 154 out of England's total of 252 in a 1991 Test against the West Indies at Headingley?

14. Who took a hat trick for England in their 2008 Test against New Zealand?

15. Australia's domestic four-day competition shares its name with which English city?

16. What nationality is the former Test umpire Rudi Koertzen?

17. Which Australian scored just 115 runs in his 250 One-Day International appearances?

18. Who smashed 115 from 57 balls in a 2007 World Twenty20 match?

19. How many teams took part in the 2012 CB 40 competition?
    a) 18
    b) 20
    c) 21

20. Which country provided the most members of the 2011 ICC World Test XI?
    a) England
    b) India
    c) South Africa

Answers to Quiz 18: India

1. 1930s
2. Anil Kumble and Kapil Dev
3. Sunil Gavaskar
4. Virender Sehwag
5. Bishan Bedi
6. Bangladesh
7. Narendra Hirwani
8. Harbhajan Singh
9. Irfan Pathan
10. R Ashwin
11. Virender Sehwag
12. John Wright
13. Anil Kumble
14. Sourav Ganguly
15. Duncan Fletcher
16. Mohammad Azharuddin
17. VVS Laxman
18. MS Dhoni
19. Zaheer Khan
20. Suresh Raina

Quiz 20: Pakistan

EASY

1. Which Pakistani holds the record for the most runs in a Test match calendar year?

2. Which spinner took 24 wickets at an average of just 14.71 in Pakistan's 2011 series against England?

3. That 2011 series against England was held in which country?

4. Who has captained Pakistan in the most Test matches?

5. What country hosted Pakistan's 2010 series against Australia?

6. Which former Sri Lanka coach took charge of the Pakistan team in March 2012?

7. True or false – Pakistan have never beaten India in a Cricket World Cup match?

8. Who captained Pakistan to victory in the 2009 World Twenty20?

9. Which all-rounder was named Man of the Match in the 2009 World Twenty20 final?

10. In which city will you find the Gaddafi Stadium?

11. Who was the leading wicket-taker in both the 2007 and 2009 World Twenty20 tournaments?

12. Wasim Akram spent the majority of his English domestic career with which county?

13. Which Pakistani holds the record for the slowest century in Test history?

14. Which left-hander has scored the most ODI hundreds for Pakistan?

15. Who are the three Pakistanis to have scored a Test match triple century?

16. Which Pakistani off spinner took 100 ODI wickets in the fewest number of games?

17. Who were the three Pakistan players jailed for their part in the 2010 spot-fixing scandal?

18. Which spinner was dismissed for a record-breaking 25 ducks between 2000 and 2010?

19. Who is Pakistan's all-time leading Test wicket-taker?
    a) Imran Khan
    b) Waqar Younis
    c) Wasim Akram

20. Who is Pakistan's all-time leading Test run-scorer?
    a) Inzamam ul Haq
    b) Javed Miandad
    c) Mohammad Yousuf

Answers to Quiz 19: Pot Luck

1. Sri Lanka
2. South Africa
3. 1948
4. Mahela Jayawardene
5. Allen Stanford
6. Billy Bowden
7. Jim Laker and Muttiah Muralitharan
8. Pakistan
9. Lasith Malinga
10. Javed Miandad
11. Amit Mishra
12. Brown Caps
13. Graham Gooch
14. Ryan Sidebottom
15. Sheffield (Shield)
16. South African
17. Glenn McGrath
18. Chris Gayle
19. 21
20. England

Quiz 21: Pot Luck

EASY

1. England all-rounder Tim Bresnan plays domestic cricket for which English county?

2. Who was the first player of Italian descent to play Test cricket for New Zealand?

3. Bangers is the nickname of which England batsman?

4. Which Pakistan-born former Middlesex, Yorkshire and Warwickshire spinner made his Test debut for South Africa in 2011?

5. Which hard-hitting batsman was nicknamed The Master Blaster?

6. Who has bowled the most overs in the history of Test cricket?

7. Narsingh Deonarine plays international cricket for which side?

8. Which county's badge features a white horse?

9. What type of delivery takes its name from the Hindi word for other?

10. The Indian Premier League is broadcast in the UK on what TV channel?

11. What colour of kit is usually worn by Pakistan in One-Day Internationals?

12. What is the name of the magazine published by the Professional Cricketers' Association?

13. Which England captain was fined over the 'dirt in the pocket' affair?

14. What flower features on the Yorkshire badge?

15. Who wrote the cricket classic Beyond A Boundary?

16. What is the vegetable of choice favoured by Geoffrey Boycott when describing bowling his mother could face?

17. Which England bowler was nicknamed the King of Spain?

18. Who are the two New Zealanders to have taken 300 Test wickets?

19. Which England player features in a TV series called Takes On The World?
    a) Andrew Flintoff
    b) Ronnie Irani
    c) Phil Tufnell

20. How many rows of stitches does the seam of a cricket ball have?
    a) 4
    b) 6
    c) 8

Answers to Quiz 20: Pakistan

1. Mohammad Yousuf
2. Saeed Ajmal
3. The United Arab Emirates
4. Imran Khan
5. England
6. Dav Whatmore
7. True
8. Younis Khan
9. Shahid Afridi
10. Lahore
11. Umar Gul
12. Lancashire
13. Mudassar Nazar
14. Saeed Anwar
15. Hanif Mohammad, Younis Khan and Inzamam ul Haq
16. Saqlain Mushtaq
17. Salman Butt, Mohammad Aamer, Mohammad Asif
18. Danish Kaneria
19. Wasim Akram
20. Javed Miandad

Quiz 22: Sri Lanka

EASY

1. Who did Sri Lanka beat in the 1996 Cricket World Cup final?

2. Who is Sri Lanka's leading Test run-scorer?

3. Who are the four Sri Lankans with 100 Test wickets?

4. Which feisty character captained Sri Lanka from 1989 to 1999?

5. Which left-arm spinner took 12 wickets in Sri Lanka's 75-run win over England in the first Test at Galle in 2012?

6. Who was the only Sri Lankan named in the 2011 ICC World Test XI?

7. Who took just 17 balls to hit a half-century in a One-Day International against Pakistan in 1996?

8. Aravinda de Silva played county cricket for which side?

9. Which India and Surrey left-arm spinner did Muttiah Muralitharan dismiss to claim his record-breaking 800th Test wicket?

10. Who scored a century for Sri Lanka in the 2011 Cricket World Cup final?

11. Who was the first Sri Lankan to score 6,000 Test runs?

12. In 2011, which Sri Lankan became the first player to take a hat trick of ODI hat tricks?

13. Which Sri Lankan mystery spinner took 6 for 16 in a T20 game against Australia in 2011?

14. Who hit a century and was named man of the match in the 1996 World Cup final?

15. Who in 1982, became the first player to score a Test century for Sri Lanka?

16. In which city will you find the R. Premadasa Stadium?

17. In what decade did Sri Lanka play their first Test match?

18. Who scored 193 in the 2011 Lord's Test, the highest score by a Sri Lankan captain at that ground?

19. Who took Sri Lanka's first, and so far only, Test hat trick in the first over of a game against Zimbabwe in 1999?
    a) Lasith Malinga
    b) Nuwan Zoysa
    c) Kumar Dharmasena

20. How many Test wickets did Muttiah Muralitharan take?
    a) 800
    b) 850
    c) 900

Answers to Quiz 21: Pot Luck

1. Yorkshire
2. Daniel Vettori
3. Marcus Trescothick
4. Imran Tahir
5. Viv Richards
6. Muttiah Muralitharan
7. West Indies
8. Kent
9. Doosra
10. ITV4
11. Green
12. All Out Cricket
13. Michael Atherton
14. A white rose
15. CLR James
16. Rhubarb
17. Ashley Giles
18. Richard Hadlee and Daniel Vettori
19. Andrew Flintoff
20. 6

Quiz 23: Pot Luck

1. Ian Botham played football for which English club?

2. Which cricketer is a team captain on TV panel show A League Of Their Own?

3. What is the only country to win the Cricket World Cup on home soil?

4. Which West Indian was Leicestershire's overseas player in 2012?

5. Who is the host of Sky Sports show Cricket Writers on TV?

6. The Gladiators is the nickname of which county's one-day team?

7. How many overs are supposed to be bowled per hour in Test cricket?

8. Which county's ground is situated at Nevil Road?

9. When told by Shane Warne that he'd been waiting two years to humiliate him again, which South African replied, 'Looks like you spent it eating'?

10. Punter is the nickname of which Australian batsman?

11. Who is the only Pakistani batsman to have scored a century of first-class centuries?

12. Which two spinners played for the World XI in the 2005 Test match against Australia?

13. Who opened the batting for England in the 2010/11 Ashes series?

14. Which Everton footballer is also the youngest player to score a century for Lancashire's 2nd XI?

15. What colour of kit do India traditionally wear in One-Day Internationals?

16. In 2011, who became became the oldest Indian to score a Test century at Lord's?

17. Mark Ramprakash has played for which two English counties?

18. The Queen's Park Oval is in which city in the Caribbean?

19. Which former England captain's two Test bowling victims were Wasim Akram and Dilip Vengsarkar?
    a) Michael Atherton
    b) Nasser Hussain
    c) Alec Stewart

20. Viv Richards and Curtly Ambrose are from which Caribbean island?
    a) Antigua
    b) Jamaica
    c) Trinidad

Answers to Quiz 22: Sri Lanka

1. Australia
2. Mahela Jayawardene
3. Muttiah Muralitharan, Chaminda Vaas, Sanath Jayasuriya, Rangana Herath
4. Arjuna Ranatunga
5. Rangana Herath
6. Kumar Sangakkara
7. Sanath Jayasuriya
8. Kent
9. Pragyan Ojha
10. Mahela Jayawardene
11. Aravinda de Silva
12. Lasith Malinga
13. Ajantha Mendis
14. Aravinda de Silva
15. Sidath Wettimuny
16. Colombo
17. 1980s
18. Tillakaratne Dilshan
19. Nuwan Zoysa
20. 800

Quiz 24: South Africa

1. Who is South Africa's all-time leading run-scorer in Test cricket?

2. The South Africans are nicknamed the proteas. What is a protea?

3. South Africa chased down a Test record fourth-innings total of 414 in 2008 against which opposition?

4. Which superstitious South African opener would tape his bat to the ceiling before each innings and made sure that every dressing room toilet seat was down before he went out to bat?

5. Who scored two double centuries in the 2003 Test series in England?

6. White Lightning was the nickname of which South African bowler?

7. Who captained South Africa on their return to Test cricket in 1991?

8. Which South African stadium is nicknamed The Bull Ring?

9. Who is South Africa's all-time leading Test wicket-taker?

10. In what year did South Africa make their World Cup debut?

11. What is the name of Morné Morkel's all-rounder brother?

12. Who captained South Africa between 1994 and 2000?

13. Which team dismissed South Africa for just 96 in the 2011 Cape Town Test?

14. The best Test bowling figures by a South African of 13 for 132 were recorded in 2005 by which bowler?

15. Which bowler did Michael Atherton describe as having an action like a 'frog in a blender'?

16. Which doughty left-handed batsman was appointed coach of the South Africa team in 2011?

17. Which left-arm spinner took 103 wickets in 37 Test matches between 2007 and 2011?

18. Who was the first non-white captain of South Africa?

19. Who holds the record for the most Test catches by a South African outfield player?
    a) Daryll Cullinan
    b) Jacques Kallis
    c) Shaun Pollock

20. Which South African reached 100 wickets in the fewest number of Tests?
    a) Allan Donald
    b) Makhaya Ntini
    c) Dale Steyn

Answers to Quiz 23: Pot Luck

1. Scunthorpe United
2. Andrew Flintoff
3. India
4. Ramnaresh Sarwan
5. Paul Allott
6. Gloucestershire
7. 15
8. Gloucestershire
9. Daryll Cullinan
10. Ricky Ponting
11. Zaheer Abbas
12. Muttiah Muralithran and Daniel Vettori
13. Alastair Cook and Andrew Strauss
14. Phil Neville
15. Blue
16. Rahul Dravid
17. Middlesex and Surrey
18. Port of Spain
19. Michael Atherton
20. Antigua

Quiz 25: Pot Luck

1. Which England all-rounder was given a 13-year prison sentence in 2009 for drug smuggling?

2. Which magazine is subtitled The Independent Voice of Cricket?

3. BooBoo was the nickname of which Gloucestershire and England all-rounder?

4. Did Test Match Special's Henry Blofeld ever play Test cricket for England?

5. Sewards was the middle name of which famous fast bowler?

6. Who is the only player to play a One-Day International for England whose surname begins with the letter Y?

7. Which cricketer was once honoured as a druid at the Welsh national Eisteddfod?

8. Who is the tallest player to play Test cricket for England?

9. World boxing champion Amir Khan is a cousin of which England bowler?

10. Parmesan Tony is an anagram of which England player's name?

11. Which Indian batsman was Derek Pringle describing when he tweeted, 'He is proof that decent and well-rounded men can excel at the highest levels of sport'?

12. Who is the only player to score a triple century and a century in the same Test match?

13. Who holds the record for the most sixes in an English first-class season?

14. Who is the only England batsman to have scored seven Test centuries before his 23rd birthday?

15. Which county's badge features a maroon Tudor rose?

16. Which film critic became President of the Lord's Taverners in 2011?

17. True or false – a batsman cannot be out LBW if the ball pitches outside leg stump?

18. At which Test venue will you find the Cathedral Road End and the River Taff End?

19. West Indian legend Clive Lloyd played county cricket for which team?
    a) Lancashire
    b) Warwickshire
    c) Yorkshire

20. Which of the following trio made the most Test appearances for Australia?
    a) Mark Waugh
    b) Steve Waugh
    c) Shane Warne

Answers to Quiz 24: South Africa

1. Jacques Kallis
2. A flower
3. Australia
4. Neil McKenzie
5. Graeme Smith
6. Allan Donald
7. Kepler Wessels
8. The Wanderers
9. Shaun Pollock
10. 1992
11. Albie Morkel
12. Hansie Cronje
13. Australia
14. Makhaya Ntini
15. Paul Adams
16. Gary Kirsten
17. Paul Harris
18. Ashwell Prince
19. Jacques Kallis
20. Dale Steyn

Quiz 26: Zimbabwe

1. In what decade did Zimbabwe make their Test debut?

2. Who is Zimbabwe's all-time leading Test run-scorer?

3. Which Zimbabwean bowler is an accomplished opera singer?

4. Which player-turned-coach was instrumental in Zimbabwe's shock win over Australia at the 1983 World Cup?

5. True or false – Graeme Hick played One-Day international cricket for Zimbabwe?

6. Who is Zimbabwe's all-time leading Test wicket-taker?

7. Who scored a century in Zimbabwe's maiden Test match and holds the record for the highest score by a Zimbabwe batsman for his 266 against Sri Lanka in 1994/95?

8. Which Zimbabwean scored an unbeaten 344 for Sussex against Somerset in 2009?

9. In which city will you find the Test venue the Queens Sports Club?

10. Can you name two Zimbabwe players whose surnames are also the names of cities in England?

11. Which Zimbabwean chicken farmer is the oldest man to have taken a hat trick in a One-Day International?

12. Which former Leicestershire and Hampshire all-rounder won three Man of the Match awards at the 1999 World Cup?

13. Which wicket-keeper made his Test debut in 2001, aged just 18?

14. What is the name of batman Andy Flower's brother who also played for Zimbabwe?

15. Which current Zimbabwe international has the same first name as a city in Canada?

16. Which fleet-footed Zimbabwean was England's fielding coach during the 2005 Ashes?

17. Which Zimbabwean all-rounder has played for Hampshire since 2005?

18. Which veteran Englishman took over as Zimbabwe coach in 2011?

19. Spinner Ray Price spent three years playing for which English county?
    a) Gloucestershire
    b) Somerset
    c) Worcestershire

20. Which team skittled Zimbabwe for their lowest-ever Test score of 51 in January 2012?
    a) Australia
    b) New Zealand
    c) South Africa

Answers to Quiz 25: Pot Luck

1. Chris Lewis
2. Spin
3. Mark Alleyne
4. No
5. Fred Trueman
6. Michael Yardy
7. Robert Croft
8. Steve Finn
9. Sajid Mahmood
10. Monty Panesar
11. Rahul Dravid
12. Graham Gooch
13. Ian Botham
14. Alastair Cook
15. Northamptonshire
16. Barry Norman
17. True
18. Cardiff's Swalec Stadium
19. Lancashire
20. Steve Waugh

Quiz 27: Pot Luck

1. Which batsman has been dismissed in the nineties the most often in Test history?

2. England seamer Chris Tremlett started his county career with which side?

3. Which Warwickshire and England batsman is the grandson of an actor who played Dr Who?

4. Which three teams took part in the 2012 CB40 competition in addition to the 18 first-class counties?

5. Which county's badge features the three Prince of Wales feathers?

6. Who is South Africa's youngest Test captain?

7. The Bearded Wonder was the nickname of which Test Match Special regular?

8. Pigeon is the nickname of which Australian bowler?

9. Who made his last Test appearance at Trent Bridge in the 2005 Ashes series?

10. Which Australian made his Test debut in the same game?

11. Which big-hitting batsman made his Test debut for England against the West Indies at Lord's in 2012?

12. Which batsman scored his 100th first-class century in 2008?

13. Seamer Jack Coles plays for which English county?

14. What was used for the first time in an ODI between Zimbabwe and England on New Year's Day 1997?

15. Which West Indian was the first player to score a century and take 5 wickets in the same One-Day International?

16. Which fixture took place for the last time at Scarborough in 1962?

17. The Dynamos is the nickname of which English county's one-day side?

18. Who captained England on the 1998/99 Ashes tour to Australia?

19. Who didn't score a century on their Test debut?
    a) Alastair Cook
    b) Kevin Pietersen
    c) Andrew Strauss

20. Who took 11 wickets in England's Test victory over Pakistan at Trent Bridge in 2010?
    a) James Anderson
    b) Stuart Broad
    c) Graeme Swann

Answers to Quiz 26: Zimbabwe

1. 1990s
2. Andy Flower
3. Henry Olonga
4. Duncan Fletcher
5. False – he was selected in the 1983 World Cup squad but didn't play
6. Heath Streak
7. Dave Houghton
8. Murray Goodwin
9. Bulawayo
10. Charles Coventry and Stuart Carlisle
11. Eddo Brandes
12. Neil Johnson
13. Tatenda Taibu
14. Grant
15. Hamilton Masakadza
16. Trevor Penney
17. Sean Ervine
18. Alan Butcher
19. Worcestershire
20. New Zealand

Quiz 28: New Zealand

1. Who is New Zealand's most prolific Test century-maker?

2. What is the nickname of the New Zealand cricket team?

3. Which New Zealander was the first man to take 400 Test wickets?

4. Who are the three New Zealanders with 5,000 Test runs?

5. In a career stretching 12 years, which New Zealander has a highest Test score of just 12 not out?

6. How many times have New Zealand reached the final of the Cricket World Cup?

7. Which Kiwi has scored 16 ODI hundreds, double the number of his closest New Zealand rival?

8. Paddles is the nickname of which New Zealand great?

9. Who was the first New Zealander to score an international T20 century?

10. Which 19-year-old seamer took five wickets in an innings on his Test debut against England in 2008?

11. Who are the two New Zealanders to have scored 4,000 ODI runs and taken 200 ODI wickets?

12. Which left-arm bowler was the leading wicket-taker at the 1999 Cricket World Cup?

13. Who took over as captain of the New Zealand Test team in November 2011?

14. Who is the youngest player to have represented New Zealand at Test cricket?

15. Which New Zealander scored the fastest double hundred in Test history?

16. Which fast bowler took 87 wickets at an average of just 22.09 in just 18 Test matches before being forced to retire through injury?

17. Which former New Zealand all-rounder is a regular in the commentary box for English county games on Sky?

18. In which city will you find a ground called The Basin Reserve?

19. What stage did the Kiwis reach in the 2011 World Cup?
    a) group stage
    b) quarterfinal
    c) semifinal

20. What colour kit did New Zealand wear at the 1992 World Cup?
    a) black
    b) grey
    c) white

Answers to Quiz 27: Pot Luck

1. Sachin Tendulkar
2. Hampshire
3. Jim Troughton
4. Scotland, The Netherlands and Unicorns
5. Surrey
6. Graeme Smith
7. Bill Frindall
8. Glenn McGrath
9. Simon Jones
10. Shaun Tait
11. Jonny Bairstow
12. Mark Ramprakash
13. Kent
14. The Duckworth-Lewis Method was used to decide a result
15. Viv Richards
16. Gentlemen versus Players
17. Durham
18. Alec Stewart
19. Kevin Pietersen
20. James Anderson

Quiz 29: Pot Luck

1. Irish spinner George Dockrell plays for which English county?

2. The Spitfires is the nickname of which English county's one-day side?

3. Pup is the nickname of which Australian Test batsman?

4. Who are the only team to lose a Test match after enforcing the follow-on?

5. Who has scored the highest Test innings for England in a losing effort?

6. Who is the most capped West Indies wicket-keeper?

7. Which English batsman scored a record 197 first-class centuries?

8. What was used for the first time in a game between the MCC and Scotland at Lord's in 2008?

9. Which spinner was the only cricketer to go on both the 1981/82 and the 1989/90 rebel tours to South Africa?

10. Which West Indian all-rounder has a daughter called Dwaynice?

11. The trophy awarded to the winners of India versus Australia Test series is named after which two batsmen?

12. Which New Zealander took a hat trick and scored a century for Gloucestershire in their 2009 Championship game against Derbyshire?

13. Rory Hamilton-Brown is the captain of which English county?

14. Levi is the nickname of which England international?

15. Who is the only New Zealander to have scored over 100 first-class centuries?

16. Which Australian had his own line of underwear called Spinners?

17. Kevin Pietersen made his Test debut against which country?

18. Who are the two Englishmen to have taken 200 Test wickets and scored over 3,000 Test runs?

19. Who wrote the book 'The Art of Captaincy'?
    a) Mike Brearley
    b) Allan Border
    c) Ricky Ponting

20. Who is the oldest player to appear in a T20 international?
    a) Rahul Dravid
    b) Brad Hogg
    c) Sanath Jayasuriya

Answers to Quiz 28: New Zealand

1. Martin Crowe
2. The Black Caps
3. Richard Hadlee
4. Martin Crowe, Stephen Fleming and John Wright
5. Chris Martin
6. Never
7. Nathan Astle
8. Richard Hadlee
9. Brendon McCullum
10. Tim Southee
11. Chris Cairns and Chris Harris
12. Geoff Allott
13. Ross Taylor
14. Daniel Vettori
15. Nathan Astle
16. Shane Bond
17. Jeremy Coney
18. Wellington
19. Semifinal
20. Grey

Quiz 30: Bangladesh

1. Bangladesh recorded their first Test victory against which country?

2. Which Australian was appointed coach of Bangladesh in 2011?

3. Who scored a century on his Test debut against India in 2000/01?

4. Who is Bangladesh's all-time leading Test run-scorer?

5. True or false – Bangladesh have beaten every Test-playing nation in a One-Day International?

6. Who made five scores of more than fifty in six Test innings against England, culminating in a century at Lord's in May 2010?

7. Which team did Bangladesh famously beat in the 1999 World Cup?

8. Who was the first Bangladeshi bowler to take seven wickets in a Test innings?

9. In which city will you find the Zahur Ahmed Chowdhury Stadium?

10. Which Test nation did Bangladesh beat at the 2007 World Twenty20?

11. Which team bowled Bangladesh out for 58 in the 2011 World Cup?

12. Which two Test-playing nations did Bangladesh beat in the 2007 Cricket World Cup?

13. In 2010, Bangladesh recorded their first win over England in England at which ground?

14. Which Australian batsman coached Bangladesh from 2007 to 2011?

15. Bangladesh recorded a famous victory over which Test-playing nation at the 2011 World Cup?

16. All-rounder Shakib al Hasan was the first Bangladeshi to play county cricket. Which team did he play for?

17. Who was the first Bangladeshi bowler to take 100 Test wickets?

18. Bangladesh earned their first ODI series win in 2010 by beating which country?

19. Whose 158 not out against India in 2004 is the highest Test score by a Bangladeshi batsman?
a) Mohammad Ashraful
b) Mahmadullah
c) Javed Omar

20. Bangladesh made their Test debut against which country?
a) India
b) Pakistan
c) Sri Lanka

Answers to Quiz 29: Pot Luck

1. Somerset
2. Kent
3. Michael Clarke
4. Australia
5. Paul Collingwood with 206 against Australia in 2006
6. Jeff Dujon
7. Jack Hobbs
8. A pink ball
9. John Emburey
10. Dwayne Bravo
11. Allan Border and Sunil Gavaskar
12. James Franklin
13. Surrey
14. Andrew Strauss
15. Glenn Turner
16. Shane Warne
17. Australia
18. Ian Botham and Andrew Flintoff
19. Mike Brearley
20. Sanath Jayasuriya

Quiz 31: Pot Luck

1. A fox features on the badge of which county?

2. Which recently departed Ashes hero is the father of Premiership rugby player Chris Pennell?

3. Which South African batsman's nickname is Biff?

4. Who are the two Indian seam bowlers with 250 Test wickets?

5. Which England international was nicknamed The Gaffer?

6. In which South African city is the Kingsmead ground?

7. Michael Vaughan played English domestic cricket for which county?

8. Which current England footballer was described by Worcestershire coach Damien D'Oliveira as 'one of the most highly-rated players in the country'?

9. When did the infamous Bodyline series take place?

10. Ronald is the middle name of which current England batsman?

11. The bearded Uncle Cricket is a famous follower of which country?

12. Which all-rounder captained the West Indies on their 2012 tour of England?

13. 'Under The Southern Cross' is an unofficial anthem of which Test team?

14. At which ground will you see a weathervane called Old Father Time?

15. Who was the first Asian player to play for Yorkshire?

16. Which county play their home games at Edgbaston?

17. How many Test wickets did Ian Botham take?

18. Shane Warne played domestic cricket in Australia for which state side?

19. Who is the only West Indian to have scored 100 first-class centuries?
    a) Brian Lara
    b) Viv Richards
    c) Garfield Sobers

20. Who holds the record for the fewest balls needed to reach a Test match triple hundred?
    a) Chris Gayle
    b) Matthew Hayden
    c) Virender Sehwag

Answers to Quiz 30: Bangladesh

1. Zimbabwe
2. Stuart Law
3. Aminul Islam
4. Habibul Bashar
5. True
6. Tamim Iqbal
7. Pakistan
8. Emanul Haque Jr
9. Chittagong
10. West Indies
11. West Indies
12. India and South Africa
13. County Ground, Bristol
14. Jamie Siddons
15. England
16. Worcestershire
17. Mohammad Rafique
18. New Zealand
19. Mohammad Ashraful
20. India

Quiz 32: T20

1. Which two countries took part in the first T20 international?

2. The first World Twenty20 took place in which country?

3. Who captained England to victory in the 2010 World Twenty20?

4. Who did England beat in the 2010 final?

5. What is the maximum number of overs a bowler can bowl in a T20 match?

6. Who smashed 16 sixes while compiling 152 from just 58 balls for Essex against Sussex in 2008?

7. Which country shocked England in the opening match of the 2009 World Twenty20?

8. Who were the winners of the first World Twenty20 in 2007?

9. Which country hosted the 2012 World Twenty20?

10. Which Irishman scored 119 from just 59 balls for Gloucestershire against Middlesex in 2011?

11. Pakistan beat which country in the final of the 2009 World Twenty20?

12. Which West Indian was the first player to score a century in a World Twenty20 game?

13. How many countries took part in the 2010 World Twenty20?

14. Who was named player of the tournament at the 2010 World Twenty20?

15. Which Indian hit six sixes in an over in the 2007 World Twenty20?

16. England used six bowlers in the final of the 2010 World Twenty20. Name them.

17. Which county won England's domestic Twenty20 competition in 2004, 2006 and 2011?

18. Which Malaysian-born spinner took 6 for 5 for Somerset against Glamorgan in a T20 game in 2011?

19. Which county won the inaugural Twenty20 Cup in England in 2003?
    a) Kent
    b) Middlesex
    c) Surrey

20. What is the name of the domestic T20 competition in Australia?
    a) Big Bash
    b) Super Thrash
    c) Monster Mash

Answers to Quiz 31: Pot Luck

1. Leicestershire
2. Graham Dilley
3. Graeme Smith
4. Kapil Dev and Zaheer Khan
5. Alec Stewart
6. Durban
7. Yorkshire
8. Joe Hart
9. 1932/33
10. Ian Bell
11. Pakistan
12. Darren Sammy
13. Australia
14. Lord's
15. Sachin Tendulkar
16. Warwickshire
17. 383
18. Victoria
19. Viv Richards
20. Virender Sehwag

Quiz 33: Pot Luck

EASY

1. Which West Indian was named Kent coach for the 2012 season?

2. Which spinning all-rounder made his Test debut for England in Sri Lanka in 2012?

3. What is the name of the trophy awarded to the winning team in Test series between Australia versus the West Indies?

4. Who was the first Yorkshire-born cricketer of Pakistani background to play for the White Rose county?

5. Who are the three post-war England batsmen to have scored three centuries in an Ashes series Down Under?

6. Which England batsman followed three successive Test ducks with three successive Test centuries between 2007 and 2009?

7. Which county won four Lord's finals in 1999 and 2000?

8. Which former Derbyshire and Sussex batsman is the cricket manager at Surrey?

9. Who was the captain of the all-conquering Warwickshire team that won three out of four domestic trophies in 1994?

10. Rhino is the nickname of which Australian fast bowler?

11. Ravi Rampaul plays international cricket for which side?

12. Who is England's second-highest Test wicket-taker?

13. Which Australian played a Test match against the West Indies in 2001 with dyed blue hair?

14. Who are the two Indian batsmen to have hit six sixes in an over?

15. Which two England players were part of the ICC World XI that took on Australia in 2005?

16. Angelo Mathews plays international cricket for which country?

17. The one-day side of which English county was formerly known as The Phoenix?

18. Which popular cricket magazine was first published in 1921?

19. Which bowler took just 1 for 150 in his first Test appearance?
    a) Anil Kumble
    b) Muttiah Muralitharan
    c) Shane Warne

20. In what city was Aussie all-rounder Andrew Symonds born?
    a) Birmingham
    b) Bombay
    c) Brisbane

Answers to Quiz 32: T20

1. Australia and New Zealand
2. South Africa
3. Paul Collingwood
4. Australia
5. Four
6. Graham Napier
7. Netherlands
8. India
9. Sri Lanka
10. Kevin O'Brien
11. Sri Lanka
12. Chris Gayle
13. 12
14. Kevin Pietersen
15. Yuvraj Singh
16. Ryan Sidebottom, Stuart Broad, Tim Bresnan, Luke Wright, Michael Yardy and Graeme Swann
17. Leicestershire
18. Arul Suppiah
19. Surrey
20. Big Bash

MEDIUM QUIZZES

Quiz 34: Pot Luck

1. Who was the first Asian player to play Test cricket for Australia?

2. Which England batsman likes to spend the off season helping out on the farm of his father-in-law?

3. Boom Boom is the nickname of which Pakistani all-rounder?

4. Which English batsman has scored seven double centuries but has never played for England?

5. Four players whose surname begins with I have won Test caps for England since 1994. Can you name them?

6. Who, in 2008, became the first England batsman to be dismissed in a Test match for 199?

7. St George's Park is a Test venue in which South African city?

8. What is the most successful bowler/wicket-keeper combination in Test history?

9. Who is the only post-war England captain to take six wickets in a Test match innings?

10. Which bowler made his first, and so far only, Test appearance for England against Bangladesh in 2010?

11. Which Australian is a patron of the French Cricket Association?

12. Which opening batsman won the Professional Cricketers' Association Player of the Year award in 2011?

13. How much does a cricket ball weigh?

14. What is the most prolific opening partnership in ODI history?

15. Which Australian state side are nicknamed the Bushrangers?

16. The Twitter handle of which former England ODI international is @colonel19?

17. Which England international plays in a band called Dr Comfort and the Lurid Revelations?

18. Which spinner was the leading Test wicket-taker in 2011?

19. Who was the first professional cricketer to receive a knighthood?
    a) Jack Hobbs
    b) Fred Trueman
    c) Herbert Sutcliffe

20. Which South African scored five centuries in the space of four Test matches in 2007?
    a) Jacques Kallis
    b) Ashwell Prince
    c) Jacques Rudolph

MEDIUM

Answers to Quiz 67: Anagrams

1.	Stuart Broad	11.	Graeme Swann
2.	Fidel Edwards	12.	Saeed Ajmal
3.	Vernon Philander	13.	Samit Patel
4.	Mahendra Singh Dhoni	14.	Brad Haddin
5.	Jesse Ryder	15.	Chris Gayle
6.	Michael Hussey	16.	Dilhara Fernando
7.	Kyle Mills	17.	Graham Onions
8.	Alastair Cook	18.	Tim Bresnan
9.	Tillakaratne Dilshan	19.	James Anderson
10.	Eoin Morgan	20.	Munaf Patel

Quiz 35: All-Rounders

1. Which current Warwickshire cricketer played in the UEFA Cup for Blackburn Rovers?

2. Who scored an unbeaten 112 then took 6-31 for England against Bangladesh in 2005?

3. Who batted on all five days of England's Test match against India in 2005/06?

4. Which Indian all-rounder was Shane Warne's first Test victim?

5. Who smashed a record-breaking 15 sixes in an ODI for Australia against Bangladesh in 2011?

6. Who are the two players to score a century and take 10 wickets in the same Test match?

7. Which all-rounder holds the record for the most consecutive ducks by an England batsman in One-Day Internationals?

8. Who are the two players to have taken over 250 ODI wickets and scored over 10,000 ODI runs?

9. In 1996, which all-rounder set the record for the highest Test innings by a number eight batsman?

10. Who is the co-host of the breakfast show on radio station TalkSport?

11. Who took 33 wickets in a three-match series against Australia in 1985?

12. Which contemporary English all-rounder has hit 16 sixes in an innings not once but twice?

13. Which all-rounder scored 210 runs at an average of 21 and took 17 wickets at an average of 28 in eight Test matches for England between 1996 and 1998?

14. England all-rounder Ben Stokes was born in which country?

15. Who scored two centuries at the 2011 World Cup and was Essex's leading first-class wicket-taker in 2008?

16. Which Surrey, Lancashire, Worcestershire and Warwickshire bowler also played in goal for Aston Villa?

17. Ian Botham had spells at which three English counties?

18. Who are the two England players to have scored a century and taken five wickets in an innings in the same Test match?

19. Which of the following all-rounders took the most Test wickets?
    a) Kapil Dev
    b) Imran Khan
    c) Richard Hadlee

20. How many five-wicket hauls did Andrew Flintoff take in Test match cricket?
    a) 3
    b) 7
    c) 12

MEDIUM

Answers to Quiz 34: Pot Luck

1. Usman Khawaja
2. Alastair Cook
3. Shahid Afridi
4. David Sales
5. Alan Igglesden, Mark Illot, Ronnie Irani and Richard Illingworth
6. Ian Bell
7. Port Elizabeth
8. Lillee and Marsh
9. Bob Willis
10. Ajmal Shahzad

11. Richie Benaud
12. Marcus Trescothick
13. 5.5 to 5.75oz (155.9g to 163g)
14. Tendulkar and Ganguly
15. Victoria
16. Phil Mustard
17. Graeme Swann
18. Saeed Ajmal
19. Sir Jack Hobbs
20. Jacques Kallis

Quiz 36: Pot Luck

1. What was the name of the 2011 film about the great West Indian team of the 1970s?

2. Which former England captain was nicknamed The Gnome?

3. Which Nobel Prize-winner played two first-class games for Dublin University in the 1920s?

4. Which current South African batsman went 78 Test innings before being dismissed for a duck?

5. Which England batsman was the second leading run-scorer in One-Day internationals in 2011?

6. Which English county plays home games at Whitgift School?

7. Who was the first player to take a One-Day International hat trick for England?

8. Which former Australian prime minister described himself as a 'cricket tragic'?

9. Who scored a century for England in the 1993 Ashes Test at Lord's?

10. In 2010, which Anguillan-born batsman became the youngest player to score a first-class century for Derbyshire?

11. Which England batsman's only score over 50 of his nine-Test career was an innings of 214 not out against India?

12. Who replaced Graeme Smith as captain of South Africa's ODI and T20 teams in 2011?

13. True or false – in the 19th century, Surrey had a player called Julius Caesar?

14. Who was the first professional to captain England?

15. Which bowler made his England Test debut in 2001 then had to wait until 2007 to win his second Test cap?

16. Which West Indian wicket-keeper scored 166 against England at the Kensington Oval in 2009?

17. Who bagged a pair and took 0 for 63 on his one and only Test appearance for England against South Africa in 1999?

18. Which current umpire took 10 wickets at an average of 21.50 in his two Test appearances for England?

19. What is the penalty if a fielder uses part of his clothing to field the ball?
    a) 4 runs
    b) 5 runs
    c) 6 runs

20. Which of this trio of England rabbits had the lowest Test batting average?
    a) Ed Giddins
    b) Devon Malcolm
    c) Phil Tufnell

Answers to Quiz 35: All-Rounders

1. Keith Barker
2. Paul Collingwood
3. Andrew Flintoff
4. Ravi Shastri
5. Shane Watson
6. Imran Khan and Ian Botham
7. Craig White
8. Sanath Jayasuriya and Jacques Kallis
9. Wasim Akram
10. Ronnie Irani
11. Richard Hadlee
12. Graham Napier
13. Mark Ealham
14. New Zealand
15. Ryan ten Doeschate
16. Jim Cumbes
17. Somerset, Worcestershire and Durham
18. Ian Botham and Tony Greig
19. Kapil Dev
20. 3

MEDIUM

Quiz 37: The Ashes

1. Which future England captain made a duck on his Test debut against Australia in 1989?

2. The first ever Ashes Test in England took place at which ground?

3. Who was David Gower's co-pilot on his ill-fated Tiger Moth flight during the 1990/91 Ashes tour?

4. True or false – Australians hold the records for the highest partnership for all ten wickets?

5. Which wicket-keeper holds the record for the most dismissals in Ashes cricket?

6. Who batted on all five days of the 1977 Trent Bridge Test?

7. Who has scored the most centuries for England in Ashes matches?

8. Which Australian bowler took over 40 wickets in both the 1981 and 1989 Ashes series?

9. Who holds the record for the most minutes at the crease without being dismissed for England against Australia?

10. Which Australian pair enjoyed a record-breaking partnership at the Gabba in 2010/11?

11. Which team dropped more catches in the 2005 Ashes series?

12. The Player of the Series in an England-versus-Australia clash receives a medal named after which pair of cricketing greats?

13. Which bowler took 10 wickets in his last Ashes Test match and never played for England again?

14. Who are the three England captains to have won Ashes series in England and Down Under?

15. Who, in 1998, was the last Englishman to take an Ashes hat trick?

16. Which member of England's 2005 Ashes-winning team was made an Honorary Citizen of Droitwich?

17. Who dismissed Don Bradman for a duck in his last Ashes innings?

18. Which batsman was left stranded on 99 not out at Perth in 1979/80 after Bob Willis was dismissed for a duck in England's second innings?

19. Who once scored a tortuous 68 from 425 deliveries?
    a) Trevor Bailey
    b) Geoff Boycott
    c) Chris Tavare

20. Which South African-born batsman was the first player to be dismissed via the third umpire?
    a) Alan Lamb
    b) Kevin Pietersen
    c) Robin Smith

MEDIUM

Answers to Quiz 36: Pot Luck

1. Fire In Babylon
2. Keith Fletcher
3. Samuel Beckett
4. AB De Villiers
5. Jonathan Trott
6. Surrey
7. James Anderson
8. John Howard
9. Graham Thorpe
10. Chesney Hughes
11. David Lloyd
12. AB de Villiers
13. True
14. Len Hutton
15. Ryan Sidebottom
16. Denesh Ramdin
17. Gavin Hamilton
18. Neil Mallender
19. 5 runs
20. Ed Giddins

Quiz 38: Pot Luck

1. Who was the first black player to play for Zimbabwe?

2. Which opener carried his bat for an unbeaten 36 from 176 balls in a 1975 World Cup game?

3. Viv Richards played in the County Championship for which two teams?

4. Which Indian scored a century in his first Test in 1984 and in his last Test in 2000?

5. Who made his England Test debut against Pakistan in 2005 at the age of 36?

6. Who scored a rapid-fire double century in a doomed fourth-innings run chase against England in 2002?

7. Which left-hander was the first batsmen to score ten One-Day International centuries for England?

8. Shane Warne dismissed which batsman the most often in Test matches?

9. Which New Zealander scored 141 not out in Worcestershire's total of 169 all out against Glamorgan in 1977?

10. In 2005, who became the first number 11 batsman to top score in a Test match for England?

11. Which West Indian took 10 wickets in a County Championship innings in 2007?

12. Which Sri Lankan opening pair put on 286 for the first wicket in a One-Day International against England in 2006?

13. Which English county plays home games at Aigburth and Stanley Park?

14. Which Englishman played his last ODI against Bangladesh in March 2011?

15. Excluding Australia, England have won the most Test matches against which country?

16. Who holds the record for the most wickets by a West Indian bowler in Test matches against England?

17. Dennis Lillee and Shane Warne are two of the three post-war Australians to take 5 wickets in an innings against England 11 times. Who is the third?

18. Who are the two bowlers to have taken 16 wickets in a Test match against England?

19. In six Test matches against Zimbabwe, how many have England won?
    a) 3
    b) 4
    c) 5

20. Which New Zealander smashed 34 from an over in a game against Oxford University in 2005?
    a) Chris Cairns
    b) Hamish Marshall
    c) Craig Spearman

Answers to Quiz 37: The Ashes

1. Michael Atherton
2. The Oval
3. John Morris
4. False – They hold nine of the ten
5. Rodney Marsh
6. Geoffrey Boycott
7. Jack Hobbs
8. Terry Alderman
9. Alastair Cook who was unbeaten for 1,022 minutes in 2010/11
10. Michael Hussey and Brad Haddin
11. England with 25 compared to Australia's 17
12. Denis Compton and Keith Miller
13. Andrew Caddick
14. Len Hutton, Mike Brearley and Andrew Strauss
15. Darren Gough
16. Ashley Giles
17. Eric Hollies
18. Geoffrey Boycott
19. Trevor Bailey
20. Robin Smith

MEDIUM

Quiz 39: England's League of Nations

Can you identify the country of birth of the following players who have represented England?

1. Craig Kieswetter

2. Colin Cowdrey

3. Dermot Reeve

4. Graeme Hick

5. Chris Lewis

6. Ted Dexter

7. Amjad Khan

8. Geraint Jones

9. Philip Defreitas

10. Tim Ambrose

11. Phil Edmonds

12. Paul Terry

13. Devon Malcolm

14. Owais Shah

15. Freddie Brown

16. Gladstone Small

17. Andrew Caddick

18. Derek Pringle

19. Sir Pelham Warner

20. Joey Benjamin

Answers to Quiz 38: Pot Luck

1. Henry Olonga
2. Sunil Gavaskar
3. Somerset and Glamorgan
4. Mohammad Azharuddin
5. Shaun Udal
6. Nathan Astle
7. Marcus Trescothick
8. Alec Stewart
9. Glenn Turner
10. Steve Harmison
11. Ottis Gibson
12. Sanath Jayasuriya and Upul Tharanga
13. Lancashire
14. Paul Collingwood
15. South Africa
16. Curtly Ambrose
17. Terry Alderman
18. Bob Massie and Muttiah Muralitharan
19. 3
20. Craig Spearman

Quiz 40: Pot Luck

1. Who was Ian Chappell describing when he said, 'If his batting was as good as Don Bradman's, he couldn't score enough runs to make up for what he costs them with his keeping'?

2. Which England nightwatchman was left stranded on 99 not out against New Zealand in 1999?

3. Which Aussie legend took 166 innings to score his maiden ODI hundred?

4. With 1,816 wickets, who is Lancashire's leading first-class wicket-taker?

5. The two stands that flank the media centre at Lord's are named after which batsmen?

6. England's fastest Test fifty was scored in just 28 balls by which batsman?

7. Who was the first cricketer to win the BBC Sports Personality of the Year award?

8. Who was the only player other than Ian Botham to score a fifty in England's second innings in the famous 1981 Headingley Ashes Test?

9. What is the narrowest margin of victory in an Ashes Test match?

10. England have lost more Test matches than they have won against which two opponents?

11. Kevin Pietersen's wife, Jessica Taylor, was a member of which band?

12. Who was the leading run-scorer in international cricket in 2011?

13. Which English county has played home games at Castle Park and Garons Park?

14. Which England player was fined in 2012 over comments made on Twitter about a TV commentator?

15. Which commentator was the subject of the aforementioned Twitter rant?

16. Who was the last English batsman to carry his bat in a Test match?

17. How many runs did VVS Laxman score during India's amazing Test victory over Australia in 2001?

18. Which West Indian scored a century on his Test debut against India in 2011?

19. Who has captained England in the most One-Day Internationals?
a) Nasser Hussain
b) Andrew Strauss
c) Michael Vaughan

20. What is the record for the most ducks in a Test match innings?
a) 5
b) 6
c) 7

MEDIUM

Answers to Quiz 39: England's League of Nations

1. South Africa
2. India
3. Hong Kong
4. Zimbabwe
5. Guyana
6. Italy
7. Denmark
8. Papua New Guinea
9. Dominica
10. Australia
11. Zambia (then Northern Rhodesia)
12. Germany
13. Jamaica
14. Pakistan
15. Peru
16. Barbados
17. New Zealand
18. Kenya
19. Trinidad
20. St Kitts

Quiz 41: Cricket World Cup

1. Which city hosted the 1996 World Cup final?

2. Who is England's leading scorer in World Cup matches?

3. Which team broke Australia's 34-game unbeaten run at the 2011 tournament?

4. Who scored an unbeaten 91 to steer India to victory in the 2011 final?

5. Who, with 74 victims, is the leading wicket-taker in World Cup history?

6. Which England bowler conceded 91 from his 10 overs against India, the most by any bowler in the 2011 competition?

7. Which Englishman scored the first century in a World Cup game?

8. Which two teams were involved in a high-scoring tie in the 2011 competition?

9. Of batsmen who have made more than 20 World Cup innings, who has the highest batting average?

10. Who took 7-20 in Australia's 2003 win over England?

11. Which pair of West Indian bowlers put on 71 for the last wicket in a group game against India in 1983?

12. Which England player left the 2011 tournament early after suffering from depression?

13. Who were the three teams to beat England in the 2011 competition?

14. Which Sri Lankan took 4 wickets in 4 balls against South Africa in 2007?

15. Who was England's leading run-scorer in the 2011 competition?

16. Which team lost 18 consecutive World Cup matches between 1983 and 1992?

17. How many teams took part in the 2011 World Cup?

18. Who, in 2011, set the record for the fastest century in World Cup history?

19. How many balls did it take him?
    a) 50
    b) 55
    c) 60

20. Who is England's leading World Cup wicket-taker?
    a) Ian Botham
    b) Mark Ealham
    c) Andrew Flintoff

Answers to Quiz 40: Pot Luck

1. Kamran Akmal
2. Alex Tudor
3. Steve Waugh
4. Brian Statham
5. Denis Compton and Bill Edrich
6. Ian Botham
7. Jim Laker
8. Graham Dilley
9. 2 runs
10. Australia and the West Indies
11. Liberty X
12. Kumar Sangakkara
13. Essex
14. Kevin Pietersen
15. Nick Knight
16. Michael Atherton
17. 281
18. Kirk Edwards
19. Andrew Strauss
20. 6

MEDIUM

Quiz 42: Pot Luck

1. Sachin Tendulkar scored his maiden Test century at which English ground?

2. Which England bowler hit his first ball in World Cup cricket for six in the final over of a game against India in 2011?

3. Which two countries took part in the first One-Day International?

4. Which nightwatchman scored an unbeaten 201 against Bangladesh in 2006?

5. The MCC's Spirit of Cricket lecture is named after which batsman?

6. Who smashed an unbeaten 45 from just 16 balls in a 2010 ODI for England against Bangladesh?

7. In 2012, Wayne Madsen was the captain of which English county?

8. Which current county coach took 21 wickets at 50.66 and scored 374 runs at 15.58 in 15 Tests for England?

9. Who took 5 wickets in an innings twice in an England career that spanned just three matches in 2003?

10. Which Australian-born batsman opened for England in three Test matches in 1995?

11. Which all-rounder did David Gower dismiss to claim his only Test wicket?

12. With the exception of Donald Bradman, who has scored the most runs in his first 25 Test appearances?

13. Which England batsman was beaten up in Cairns on England's 1998/99 Ashes tour?

14. Which Indian was the man of the match in the 1983 World Cup final?

15. Which seam bowler was the first player born in the 1990s to play Test cricket?

16. Former Glamorgan captain David Hemp played international cricket for which country?

17. What is the name of the award-winning novel by Joseph O'Neill about a cricket-playing Dutch expatriate?

18. Who was the first English-born black player to play Test cricket for England?

19. What is England's highest Test score?
    a) 893 for 7
    b) 903 for 7
    c) 913 for 7

20. Who were England's opponents when they compiled that mammoth score?
    a) Australia
    b) Bangladesh
    c) South Africa

Answers to Quiz 41: Cricket World Cup

1. Lahore
2. Graham Gooch
3. Pakistan
4. MS Dhoni
5. Glenn McGrath
6. James Anderson
7. Dennis Amiss
8. England and India
9. Viv Richards
10. Andy Bichel
11. Andy Roberts and Joel Garner
12. Michael Yardy
13. Ireland, Bangladesh and Sri Lanka
14. Lasith Malinga
15. Jonathan Trott
16. Zimbabwe
17. 14
18. Kevin O'Brien
19. 50
20. Ian Botham

MEDIUM

Quiz 43: Grounds and Stadiums

1. Excluding Lord's, which English ground has hosted the most Test matches?

2. In which city will you find the Wankhede Stadium?

3. Don Bradman scored two Test triple centuries at which English ground?

4. Eden Park is in which city?

5. A wind called the Fremantle Doctor can affect conditions at which Test ground?

6. Which ground hosted the first Test match in the West Indies?

7. Brian Lara twice broke the world record for the highest individual Test score at which ground?

8. What is the name of the Test match ground in Bridgetown, Barbados?

9. At which ground can you sit in the RES Wyatt Stand?

10. What is the name of the giant red conference and events centre at Old Trafford?

11. England were dismissed for just 46 in 1994 at which West Indian ground?

12. The Randwick End and the Paddington End are features of which Test match venue?

13. Old Trafford's Warwick Road End was renamed in honour of which bowler?

14. Where will you find the Bellerive Oval?

15. What is the name of the ground overlooked by Table Mountain?

16. England retained the 2010/11 Ashes at which ground?

17. Which county play home games at The St Lawrence Ground?

18. The Finchale End and the Lumley End are at which English ground?

19. Why was the West Indies v England Test at Antigua in 2009 abandoned after only 10 deliveries?
    a) there was a huge crack in the pitch
    b) the pitch was vandalised
    c) the run ups were unsuitable for the bowlers

20. Bourda was a Test match venue in which country?
    a) Dominica
    b) Guyana
    c) St Kitts

MEDIUM

Answers to Quiz 42: Pot Luck

1. Old Trafford
2. Ajmal Shahzad
3. England and Australia
4. Jason Gillespie
5. Colin Cowdrey
6. Ravi Bopara
7. Derbyshire
8. David Capel
9. Richard Johnson
10. Jason Gallian
11. Kapil Dev
12. Kevin Pietersen
13. John Crawley
14. Mohinder Amarnath
15. Mohammad Amir
16. Bermuda
17. Netherland
18. David Lawrence
19. 903 for 7
20. Australia

Quiz 44: Pot Luck

1. How many Cricket World Cups did Sachin Tendulkar take part in?

2. Which sport at the 2012 Olympics was hosted at Lord's?

3. Which veteran Worcestershire seamer was named one of Wisden's Five Cricketers of the Year in 2012?

4. Kingsmead is a Test match venue in which South African city?

5. Which cricket-loving comedian released the 1985 song N-N-Nineteen Not Out?

6. Who took a Test hat trick for England against India in 2011?

7. Which country had to wait 26 years for their first Test match win?

8. Who holds the record for the highest Test innings by a wicket-keeper?

9. Which England bowler took 177 Test wickets at an average of 27.32 in 46 matches between 1989 and 1998?

10. Who is the only Zimbabwean to have taken 200 Test wickets?

11. Who, in 2001, became only the second player to play Test cricket for England whose surname contains the letter Z?

12. Which New Zealander reached 50 by hitting 13 fours and a single in an innings of 53 for Middlesex in 2005?

13. Matches in the first Cricket World Cup were how many overs a side?

14. Which cricketer won the BBC Sports Personality of the Year award in 1975?

15. Who was the leading Test match run-scorer in 2011?

16. What nationality is Gloucestershire all-rounder Kane Williamson?

17. Hendrik Human are the real first names of which South African batsman?

18. Arundel Castle is a venue sometimes used by which English county?

19. How many Test matches did the West Indies lose against England between 1973 and 1988?
    a) 0
    b) 1
    c) 2

20. Which batsman, not known for his fast scoring, holds the record for the highest score in a county limited overs final at Lord's?
    a) Geoffrey Boycott
    b) Chris Tavare
    c) Jonathan Trott

Answers to Quiz 43: Grounds and Stadiums

1. The Oval
2. Mumbai
3. Headingley
4. Auckland
5. The WACA in Perth
6. The Kensington Oval
7. Antigua Recreation Ground
8. Kensington Oval
9. Edgbaston
10. The Point
11. The Queen's Park Oval in Trinidad
12. The Sydney Cricket Ground
13. Brian Statham
14. Hobart, Tasmania
15. Newlands
16. The MCG
17. Kent
18. Durham's Riverside
19. The run ups were unsuitable for the bowlers
20. Guyana

MEDIUM

Quiz 45: Captains

1. Who was the first black captain of the West Indies?

2. Which four men captained England during their ill-fated 1988 series against the West Indies?

3. Michael Vaughan resigned as England Test captain after a defeat at the hands of which country?

4. Who captained England in their 2011 ODI against Ireland in Dublin?

5. How many matches did Mike Gatting win as England captain?

6. Which Zimbabwean is the youngest player to captain a Test team?

7. True or false – Shane Warne never captained Australia in an international match?

8. Which Lancashire captain won the Man of the Match award in the 1984 B&H Cup final despite scoring a duck and not bowling?

9. Which county has provided England with the most Test captains?

10. Who was the first man to captain England in a T20 international?

11. Who was the first captain to forfeit a Test match?

12. Which two men captained England rebel tours to South Africa?

13. Who captained Durham to the County Championship title in 2009?

14. Who captained England for the first time in 1968 at the age of 41?

15. Who was the first captain to forfeit an innings in a Test match?

16. The Premier League in the 21st century was the chosen specialised subject of which former England captain on Celebrity Mastermind?

17. Who captained Surrey to promotion from Division Two of the County Championship in 2011?

18. Who captained Ireland at the 2010 World Twenty20 and the 2011 World Cup?

19. How many tosses did Mark Taylor win in the five-match 1998/99 Ashes series?
    a) 0
    b) 4
    c) 5

20. Which of the following trio won the most Test matches as England captain?
    a) Ian Botham
    b) Andrew Flintoff
    c) Kevin Pietersen

MEDIUM

Answers to Quiz 44: Pot Luck

1. Six
2. Archery
3. Alan Richardson
4. Durban
5. Rory Bremner
6. Stuart Broad
7. New Zealand
8. Andy Flower
9. Angus Fraser
10. Heath Streak
11. Usman Afzaal
12. Scott Styris
13. 60
14. David Steele
15. Rahul Dravid
16. New Zealander
17. Boeta Dippenaar
18. Sussex
19. 0
20. Geoffrey Boycott

Quiz 46: Pot Luck

1. In what country do teams compete for the Plunket Shield?

2. Which batsman smashed 41 from just 21 balls to steer England to victory in his ODI debut against India in 2011?

3. Which England bowler took 297 Test wickets for England between 1966 and 1982?

4. Who holds the record for the highest score by a visiting captain in a Test match at Lord's?

5. Who was named in the squad for four of England's five 2005 Ashes matches but didn't play a game?

6. Which two bowlers have taken over 500 ODI wickets?

7. Which Middlesex player has the same name as a member of Take That?

8. Who is England's leading ODI wicket-taker?

9. Which Aussie spinner took 5 for 34 on his Test debut against Sri Lanka in Galle in 2011?

10. Which English batsman's only Test century was an innings of 221 against West Indies in 2004?

11. England's biggest Test win, by an innings and 579, came against which country?

12. In the 2005 Ashes series, who did Steve Harmison dismiss to seal a narrow win in the Edgbaston Test?

13. Which team recorded their first win over Australia in 26 years in 2011?

14. Who succeeded Anthony McGrath as captain of Yorkshire in 2010?

15. The prolific batsman Archie MacLaren played for which English county?

16. The annual fixture between the Indian domestic champions and the Rest of India XI shares its name with the surname of which former England international?

17. Who holds the record for the most wickets in a Test series against England?

18. Who are the four West Indian batsmen to have scored 8,000 ODI runs?

19. What is England's lowest Test score?
    a) 45
    b) 46
    c) 47

20. Who dismissed them for that dismal score?
    a) Australia
    b) South Africa
    c) West Indies

Answers to Quiz 45: Captains

1. George Headley
2. Mike Gatting, Chris Cowdrey, John Emburey and Graham Gooch
3. South Africa
4. Eoin Morgan
5. 2
6. Tatenda Taibu
7. False
8. John Abrahams
9. Middlesex
10. Michael Vaughan
11. Inzamam ul Haq
12. Graham Gooch and Mike Gatting
13. Will Smith
14. Tom Graveney
15. Hansie Cronje
16. Michael Vaughan
17. Rory Hamilton-Brown
18. William Porterfield
19. 5
20. Andrew Flintoff with two

Quiz 47: Family Ties

1. Which West Indian legend is the cricketing grandfather of Lancashire's Kyle Hogg?

2. Can you name the two brothers, one of whom has played Test cricket for England, the other Test cricket for Australia?

3. What is the name of Graeme Swann's brother, who played county cricket for Northamptonshire and Lancashire?

4. Chris Tremlett's father and grandfather both played first-class cricket. What are their names?

5. Pedro Collins is the half-brother of which West Indian paceman?

6. Which member of a famous cricketing family took 5 for 85 on his Test debut for New Zealand in 2011?

7. Which former Australian opener's son scored a century on his Test debut against Sri Lanka in 2011?

8. What are the first names of Gloucestershire's Gidman brothers?

9. Which brothers played together in the same County Championship and FA Cup winning sides?

10. Who are the two father-and-son combinations to have taken 100 Test wickets?

11. Richard Hadlee's brother also played international cricket for New Zealand. What is his name?

12. Australian Darren Lehmann is the brother-in-law of which England all-rounder?

13. Who were the first identical twins to play Test cricket?

14. Which father and son played 15 and 18 Tests respectively for England before both of their careers were curtailed by injury?

15. The father of which England international played football for Manchester United and Huddersfield Town?

16. Three members of which family have kept wicket for Pakistan since 2010?

17. Which brothers played for Ireland in the 2011 Cricket World Cup?

18. Which brothers played for New Zealand in the same tournament?

19. How are Dwayne and Darren Bravo related?
    a) half brothers
    b) cousins
    c) uncle and nephew

20. Which Chappell brother bowled the infamous underarm delivery at the end of an ODI against New Zealand?
    a) Greg
    b) Ian
    c) Trevor

MEDIUM

Answers to Quiz 46: Pot Luck

1. New Zealand
2. Jonny Bairstow
3. Derek Underwood
4. Graeme Smith
5. Chris Tremlett
6. Muttiah Muralitharan and Wasim Akram
7. Robbie Williams
8. Darren Gough
9. Nathan Lyon
10. Robert Key
11. Australia
12. Michael Kasprowicz
13. New Zealand
14. Andrew Gale
15. Lancashire
16. Irani
17. Terry Alderman
18. Brian Lara, Shivnarine Chanderpaul, Desmond Haynes and Chris Gayle
19. 45
20. Australia

Quiz 48: Pot Luck

MEDIUM

1. What is England's most prolific opening partnership in Test cricket?

2. Who took a hat trick for England against the West Indies in Bridgetown, Barbados in 2004?

3. Australia's highest-ever Test score of 758 for 8 declared was made against which side?

4. Other than Jim Laker, who is the only man to take all ten wickets in a Test match innings?

5. When Garfield Sobers hit six sixes in an over in 1968, who was the unfortunate bowler?

6. Which cricket writer's works include The Summer Game, Good Days, Full Score and Close of Play?

7. Who were named Wisden's five cricketers of the 20th century?

8. Who was the only Indian to score a Test century in India's ill-fated tour of England in 2011?

9. Indian sportsmanship reprieved which England batsman who had been legitimately, if controversially run out at Trent Bridge in 2011?

10. Which cricketer made the money at the Aussie Millions poker tournament in 2010?

11. Which Glamorgan and Kent batsman has the same name as a former long jump World Champion?

12. Which St Vincent-born seamer, whose middle name was Fitzgerald, played one Test for England against India in 1990?

13. Who is the youngest player to play Test cricket for England?

14. Who holds the record for the most consecutive Test appearances?

15. Which Surrey batsman was dismissed for obstructing the field against Gloucestershire in 2011?

16. Which Hampshire pair put on a mammoth 523 for the third wicket against Yorkshire in 2011?

17. Who is Pakistan's youngest Test match captain?

18. West Indian legend Clive Lloyd is from which country?

19. How old was Sachin Tendulkar when he scored his first Test century?
    a) 16
    b) 17
    c) 18

20. Kevin Pietersen was England Test captain for how many matches?
    a) 1
    b) 2
    c) 3

Answers to Quiz 47: Family Ties

1. Sonny Ramadhin
2. Darren and James Pattinson
3. Alec Swann
4. Tim and Maurice
5. Fidel Edwards
6. Doug Bracewell
7. Geoff Marsh (his son is Shaun Marsh)
8. Alex and Will
9. Denis and Les Compton
10. Lance and Chris Cairns and Peter and Shaun Pollock
11. Barry
12. Craig White
13. Hamish and James Marshall
14. Jeff and Simon Jones
15. Ryan Sidebottom – his father is Arnie Sidebottom
16. The Akmal family
17. Niall and Kevin O'Brien
18. Nathan and Brendon McCullum
19. They're half-brothers
20. Trevor

Quiz 49: The Men in White Coats

1. Who was the first umpire to stand in 100 Test matches?

2. Which umpire called Muttiah Muralitharan for throwing at the Melbourne Test in 1995?

3. Who was the first umpire to stand in 200 One-Day Internationals?

4. Which former Australian fast bowler made his on-field ODI umpiring debut in 2009?

5. Who were the two Englishmen on the 2012 Elite Panel of Umpires?

6. Which former Durham batsman was named PCA Umpire of the Year in 2011 and is the youngest person to umpire in first-class cricket?

7. Who was the first man to referee in football's Premier League and in first-class cricket?

8. Which English umpire resigned from international cricket after Australia's Test against the West Indies in 2009?

9. Which current first-class umpire played 232 first-class matches for Warwickshire, Yorkshire and Hampshire?

10. Who was the only Sri Lankan on the 2012 Elite Panel of Umpires?

11. Slow Death was the title of which umpire's autobiography?

12. Which Australian stood in 95 Test matches between 1998 and 2011?

13. Which current English umpire took a wicket with his first ball in Test cricket?

14. Which ghostly umpire likes to listen to heavy metal music before going out to umpire?

15. What nationality is Marais Erasmus?

16. Which Australian batsman made his debut as an ICC match referee in 2011?

17. Which current umpire, who played for Gloucestershire and Somerset, was born in Penang, Malaysia?

18. What decision is given when an umpire places his right hand on his left shoulder?

19. Who is the author of the book that is considered the bible of umpiring?
    a) John Smith
    b) Ron Smith
    c) Tom Smith

20. Which English umpire stood in the most Test matches?
    a) Dickie Bird
    b) Charlie Elliott
    c) David Shepherd

Answers to Quiz 48: Pot Luck

1. Andrew Strauss and Alastair Cook
2. Matthew Hoggard
3. West Indies
4. Anil Kumble
5. Malcolm Nash
6. Neville Cardus
7. Don Bradman, Jack Hobbs, Viv Richards, Shane Warne and Garfield Sobers
8. Rahul Dravid
9. Ian Bell
10. Shane Warne
11. Mike Powell
12. Neil Williams
13. Brian Close
14. Allan Border
15. Mark Ramprakash
16. Michael Carberry and Neil McKenzie
17. Waqar Younis
18. Guyana
19. 17
20. 3

MEDIUM

Quiz 50: Pot Luck

1. Which swing bowler was India's leading wicket-taker in their 2011 Test series against England?

2. Which country made their Test debut in 1982?

3. Don Bradman played Test cricket against which four countries?

4. Who are the four West Indians to have scored Test match triple centuries?

5. Who holds the record for the highest Test innings by a South African batsman?

6. How old was Sachin Tendulkar when he made his Test debut?

7. Who is the West Indies' most capped Test player?

8. Which England batsman smashed a window in the dressing room at Lord's after being run out against Sri Lanka in 2011?

9. What trophy is awarded each year to the scorer of the fastest century in county cricket?

10. Who did Jonathan Agnew succeed as the BBC's cricket correspondent?

11. Which batsman holds the record for the most first-class hundreds at Canterbury?

12. Which Somerset pair put on opening stands of over 200 in both innings of their 2011 County Championship game against Yorkshire at Taunton?

13. Whose one and only game as England Test captain was a 1999 draw against New Zealand?

14. Where are the headquarters of the ICC?

15. Who, in May 2011, was named ECB Men's Cricketer of the Year?

16. Which former England international is the great nephew of the creator of James Bond?

17. Which Australian scored 839 runs in the 1989 Ashes series?

18. Which England cricketer was awarded the 2006 Beard of the Year award?

19. What was Donald Bradman's middle name?
    a) George
    b) Gregory
    c) Graham

20. Which South African seamer needed just 37 innings to take his first 100 Test wickets?
    a) Allan Donald
    b) Makhaya Ntini
    c) Dale Steyn

Answers to Quiz 49: The Men in White Coats

1. Steve Bucknor
2. Darrell Hair
3. Rudi Koertzen
4. Paul Reiffel
5. Ian Gould and Richard Kettleborough
6. Michael Gough
7. Martin Bodenham
8. Mark Benson
9. Peter Hartley
10. Kumar Dharmasena
11. Rudi Koertzen
12. Daryl Harper
13. Richard Illingworth
14. Neil Mallender
15. South African
16. David Boon
17. Jeremy Lloyds
18. He's awarded the fielding team 5 penalty runs
19. Tom Smith
20. David Shepherd

MEDIUM

Quiz 51: Corpulent Cricketers

1. Which 18-stone policeman took a stunning one-handed catch for Bermuda in the 2007 World Cup?

2. Who was described by Wasim Akram as the best death bowler in county cricket in the late 1990s?

3. Despite scoring 500 runs in a Shield season, which South Australia and Glamorgan batsman was dumped by his state side for being too fat?

4. Which hefty Pakistani batsman dismissed Brian Lara with his first ball in ODI cricket?

5. Which Australian skipper was nicknamed The Big Ship?

6. Which chunky England bowler was a team captain on the TV show Hole In The Wall?

7. Which New Zealand batsman scored his maiden Test double century against India in 2008/09?

8. Who was sent emergency supplies of baked beans and spaghetti hoops on a tour to India in 1998?

9. Which well-built Australian wicket-keeper, who played 19 Tests from 1959 to 1969, went on to become one of the first international match referees?

10. Which Warwickshire batsman scored over 15,000 first-class runs at an average of 40.07 but never played for England?

11. Who, when asked why he was so fat by Glenn McGrath, replied, 'Because every time I make love to your wife she gives me a biscuit'?

12. Which off-spinning all-rounder played two Tests and 31 ODIs for India between 2004 and 2007?

13. Which bowler appeared on the Australian version of Celebrity Fit Club and was the face of the All Bran diet?

14. Which Sri Lankan asked for a runner in an ODI in Sydney was told by Ian Healy, 'You don't get a runner for being an overweight, unfit, fat ****!'?

15. Which all-rounder was described by Kevin Pietersen in 2009 as being 'fat, unfit and lazy'?

16. Which Devon-born batsman played 16 Tests and 85 ODIs for New Zealand between 1995 and 2001?

17. Who took 985 first-class wickets for Lancashire and captained Tasmania to their first win in a Sheffield Shield match?

18. Which beefy Australian middle order batsman made 30 Test appearances between 1982 and 1987?

19. Boof was the nickname of which sturdy Australian batsman?
    a) David Boon
    b) Darren Lehmann
    c) Mark Taylor

20. Which big-hitting batsman hit the longest six at the 2011 World Cup?
    a) Kevin O'Brien
    b) Samit Patel
    c) David Warner

Answers to Quiz 50: Pot Luck

1. Praveen Kumar
2. Sri Lanka
3. England, South Africa, India and West Indies
4. Brian Lara, Garfield Sobers, Chris Gayle and Lawrence Rowe
5. AB De Villiers
6. 16
7. Shivnarine Chanderpaul
8. Matt Prior
9. The Walter Lawrence Trophy
10. Christopher Martin-Jenkins
11. Rob Key
12. Marcus Trescothick and Arul Suppiah
13. Mark Butcher
14. Dubai
15. Jonathan Trott
16. Matthew Fleming
17. Mark Taylor
18. Monty Panesar
19. George
20. Dale Steyn

MEDIUM

Quiz 52: Pot Luck

1. Who were the first three left-arm bowlers to take 300 Test wickets?

2. Who was the only Englishman named in the ICC World One-day team in 2011?

3. Which cricketer is the co-host of the drive time show on radio station Talk Sport?

4. Three England batsmen scored over 400 runs in the 2005 Ashes series. Can you name them?

5. Who has dismissed the most Australian batsmen in Test match cricket?

6. Which bowler took his 500th first-class wicket on England's 2012 tour of Sri Lanka?

7. Which bowler claimed his 300th first-class wicket on the same tour?

8. Who wrote the award-winning book A Lot of Hard Yakka?

9. Which Indian carried his bat in the 2011 Oval Test against England?

10. Who, after watching Alastair Cook's mammoth innings of 294 at Edgbaston in 2011 tweeted, 'This is the grand final of the worst Test day's play I have ever watched'?

11. Which Sri Lankan Test ground was destroyed by the 2004 tsunami?

12. Which number 11 batsman scored a crucial 16 from 15 balls to help England to victory over Australia in the 1998 Melbourne Test?

13. Which former England seam bowler is the cricket correspondent at The Guardian?

14. Who played more Test matches for England – Graeme Hick or Mark Ramprakash?

15. Which England player got sunstroke after shaving his head before a match in the Caribbean?

16. The youngest diocesan bishop of the Church of England also played Test cricket for England. What was his name?

17. Which England batsman has been run out more often than any other in Test cricket?

18. Who were the first four England batsmen to score over 8,000 Test runs?

19. How many of Tim Bresnan's first ten Test match appearances resulted in England winning by an innings?
    a) 3
    b) 4
    c) 5

20. Which Australian took the most Test wickets out of
    a) Terry Alderman
    b) Merv Hughes
    c) Jeff Thomson

MEDIUM

Answers to Quiz 51: Corpulent Cricketers

1. Dwayne Leverock
2. Ian Austin
3. Mark Cosgrove
4. Inzamam ul Haq
5. Warwick Armstrong
6. Darren Gough
7. Jesse Ryder
8. Shane Warne
9. Barry Jarman
10. Andy Moles
11. Eddo Brandes
12. Ramesh Powar
13. Merv Hughes
14. Arjuna Ranatunga
15. Samit Patel
16. Roger Twose
17. Jack Simmons
18. Greg Ritchie
19. Darren Lehmann
20. Kevin O'Brien

Quiz 53: County Cricket

1. Who is the only batsman to have scored a triple century in three different decades?

2. Which seamer took his 800th first-class wicket playing for Surrey against Sussex in April 2012?

3. Who were the only two teams that didn't win the Sunday League?

4. Which all-rounder top scored in both of Warwickshire's innings against Hampshire in a 2011 Championship match and took 10 wickets but still ended up on the losing side?

5. Which West Indian scored his 12,000th first-class run during a 2012 Championship match between Derbyshire and Leicestershire?

6. Who was the leading overseas wicket-taker in the County Championship in 2011?

7. Which Australian all-rounder was the first player to score a century in English domestic T20 cricket?

8. Who captained Nottinghamshire to County Championship victory in 2010?

9. Which New Zealand all-rounder was the only player to take 10 wickets in a match twice in the 2011 County Championship?

10. Who was the last man to take 100 wickets and score 1,000 runs in an English first-class season?

11. Which West Indian topped the 2011 County Championship batting averages?

12. Which spinner took the most County Championship wickets in 2011?

13. Which first-class county were bowled out for just 58 by Leeds/Bradford MCCU in 2012?

14. Which Surrey and England bowler was the leading wicket-taker in the 2011 Clydesdale Bank 40 competition?

15. Which South African was the leading run-scorer in Division Two of the 2011 County Championship?

16. Which Nottinghamshire all-rounder picked up his 500th first-class wicket against Somerset in April 2012?

17. Which county won their only championship in 1936?

18. Which county captain is the cousin of actor Harry Melling from the Harry Potter films?

19. Which team scored a mammoth 399 for 4 in a 40 over game against Worcestershire in 2011?
    a) Surrey
    b) Sussex
    c) Warwickshire

20. Which Kent all-rounder holds the record for the fastest century in a 40-over game?
    a) Mark Ealham
    b) Matthew Fleming
    c) Andrew Symonds

Answers to Quiz 52: Pot Luck

1. Chaminda Vaas, Daniel Vettori and Wasim Akram
2. Graeme Swann
3. Darren Gough
4. Kevin Pietersen, Marcus Trescothick and Andrew Flintoff
5. Ian Botham
6. James Anderson
7. Tim Bresnan
8. Simon Hughes
9. Rahul Dravid
10. Shane Warne
11. Galle
12. Alan Mullally
13. Mike Selvey
14. Graeme Hick
15. Chris Lewis
16. David Sheppard
17. Geoffrey Boycott
18. Graham Gooch, Alec Stewart, David Gower and Geoffrey Boycott
19. 5
20. Merv Hughes

MEDIUM

Quiz 54: Pot Luck

MEDIUM

1. Which current Sussex player's father and uncle both played international cricket for England?

2. Which English ground shares its name with a venue that has hosted American football's Super Bowl?

3. Nasser Hussain and Andrew Strauss both attended which university?

4. The Sea End and the Cromwell Road End can be found at which English county ground?

5. Which team dismissed Durham MCC University for just 18 in a first-class match in 2012?

6. Who has won the most Test match Player of the Match awards for England?

7. Which England player recorded a saxophone solo for the BBC children's animated series Freefonix?

8. What was the venue for the 2007 World Cup final?

9. Which fielder took 12 catches for England in the 1981 Ashes series?

10. Who are the two England bowlers to have taken six wickets in a One-Day International for England?

11. Which all-rounder played One-Day Internationals for both England and Scotland and also coached Namibia in the 2003 World Cup?

12. Which country beat the West Indies by 9 wickets after bowling them out for just 25 in a 1969 game?

13. Who twice took 8 wickets in a Test innings for England on tours of the West Indies in 1994 and 1998?

14. Ian Botham's Test best bowling figures of 8 for 34 came against which opposition?

15. Who took the catch that secured the 1986/87 Ashes for England?

16. Who is England's most capped one-day player?

17. Monty Panesar was the first Sikh to play for England. Who was the second?

18. True or false – no innings in Test history has ever seen all ten batsmen bowled?

19. Which of the following all-rounders took the most Test wickets?
    a) Ian Botham
    b) Imran Khan
    c) Kapil Dev

20. What was Don Bradman's highest first-class score?
    a) 432 not out
    b) 442 not out
    c) 452 not out

Answers to Quiz 53: County Cricket

1. Graeme Hick
2. Jon Lewis
3. Durham and Northants
4. Chris Woakes
5. Ramnaresh Sarwan
6. Chaminda Vaas
7. Ian Harvey
8. Chris Read
9. Andre Adams
10. Franklyn Stephenson
11. Shivnarine Chanderpaul
12. Monty Panesar
13. Sussex
14. Jade Dernbach
15. Zander de Bruyn
16. Paul Franks
17. Derbyshire
18. Jim Troughton
19. Sussex
20. Mark Ealham

MEDIUM

Quiz 55: Spinners

1. Which Pakistani spinner fought with a spectator during a Test match in Barbados in 1988?

2. Which leg spinner took the most Test wickets for the West Indies in 2011?

3. Which spinner was the last bowler to take 100 wickets in a County Championship season?

4. Excluding Shane Warne, who is Australia's leading spinner in Test cricket?

5. Of bowlers who have taken 20 Test wickets, which spinner has the the highest average?

6. Who was the first English spinner to take 50 Test wickets in a calendar year?

7. Who were England's two specialist spinners during the 2002/03 Ashes tour?

8. Jim Laker famously took 19 wickets in a 1953 Ashes Test. Who took the other wicket?

9. Who took 147 wickets for England in a Test career that stretched from 1978 to 1995?

10. Which Indian took more Test wickets, 242, than he scored runs, 167?

11. Which Australian spinner has the same name as an Olympic medal-winning British high jumper?

12. Who took 208 Test wickets in 44 Tests for Australia between 1998 and 2008?

13. Which Australian was the subject of Gideon Haigh's award winning book 'Mystery Spinner'?

14. Which spinner took 2 for 39 on his One-Day International debut for England against Pakistan in 2011?

15. What was the nickname of Australian leggie Bill O'Reilly?

16. Which spinner made his England debut in a one-day international against Ireland in August 2011?

17. With 307 Test wickets, who is the leading West Indian spin bowler?

18. Which leg spin guru died in 2011 at the age of 66?

19. Which Australian spinner won a World Cup winner's medal in 2003, even though he didn't play a single game in the competition?
    a) Nathan Hauritz
    b) Jason Krejza
    c) Stuart MacGill

20. Which Pakistani is credited with inventing the doosra?
    a) Abdul Qadir
    b) Mushtaq Ahmed
    c) Saqlain Mushtaq

Answers to Quiz 54: Pot Luck

1. Luke Wells
2. The Rose Bowl
3. Durham
4. The County Ground, Hove
5. Durham
6. Ian Botham
7. Alastair Cook
8. Kensington Oval, Barbados
9. Ian Botham
10. Paul Collingwood and Chris Woakes
11. Dougie Brown
12. Ireland
13. Angus Fraser
14. Pakistan
15. Gladstone Small
16. Paul Collingwood
17. Ravi Bopara
18. True
19. Kapil Dev
20. 452 not out

MEDIUM

Quiz 56: Pot Luck

1. Which English batsman was the only player to average over 100 in Tests in 2011?

2. In what decade did Leicestershire win their first County Championship and their first one-day trophies?

3. Who is the cricket correspondent for radio station Talk Sport?

4. Who succeeded Viv Richards as the captain of the West Indies?

5. Which England batsman reached 8,000 Test runs in the fewest number of innings?

6. Which former England batsman, whose middle name is Arnold, was nicknamed Judge?

7. Which county represented England in the 2011 Champions League T20?

8. 2005 Ashes hero Simon Jones has played for which three counties?

9. Allan Donald played in England for which two English counties?

10. Which England player was forced to apologise after making an expletive-ridden rant at a fellow Twitter user in 2009?

11. Who took 5 wickets at an average of 27 in his only Test appearance for England against South Africa in 2003?

12. What was Viv Richards' highest Test score?

13. Which Indian bowled a beamer at Kevin Pietersen in the 2007 Trent Bridge Test?

14. David Johnson played two Test matches in 1996 for which country?

15. Which franchise did Kevin Pietersen play for in the 2012 edition of the Indian Premier League?

16. The sister of which member of the England squad works for the team as an analyst?

17. St Aubrun is the middle name of which cricketer?

18. Which three teams took part in World Series Cricket?

19. Who has scored the most Test runs for England without ever reaching 50?
    a) Andrew Caddick
    b) Fred Trueman
    c) Bob Willis

20. Which Italian football giant was originally founded as a cricket and football club?
    a) AC Milan
    b) Inter Milan
    c) Juventus

Answers to Quiz 55: Spinners

1. Abdul Qadir
2. Devendra Bishoo
3. Mushtaq Ahmed
4. Richie Benaud with 248 wickets
5. Ian Salisbury
6. Graeme Swann
7. Ashley Giles and Richard Dawson
8. Tony Lock
9. John Emburey
10. Bhagwat Chandrasekhar
11. Steve Smith
12. Stuart MacGill
13. Jack Iverson
14. Danny Briggs
15. Tiger
16. Scott Borthwick
17. Lance Gibbs
18. Terry Jenner
19. Nathan Hauritz
20. Saqlain Mushtaq

Quiz 57: Pacemen

1. Which West Indian took an amazing 7 wickets for just 1 run in a devastating spell against Australia in 1992/93?

2. Frank Tyson played county cricket for which team?

3. Which extremely quick Australian retired from ODI cricket in 2011 at the age of just 28?

4. Which fearsome fast bowler owned a Blackpool sweetshop after retiring from cricket?

5. Who described the thought process behind his bowling as, 'I just run in and go whang'?

6. Eugene is the middle name of which erratic but sometimes brilliant former England paceman?

7. Which South African was named ICC Cricketer of the Year in 2008?

8. Who, in 2012, became the first West Indian in seven years to take 10 wickets in a Test match?

9. Which Sri Lankan was smashed for 96 runs from just 7.4 overs against India in Hobart in February 2012?

10. Who was the first player with Aboriginal ancestry to play Test cricket for Australia?

11. Which West Indian quick took five wickets on his Test debut against Sri Lanka in 2003?

12. Who did Steve Harmison dismiss with a fiendish slower ball on the penultimate day of the 2005 Ashes Test at Edgbaston?

13. Which Australian fast bowler also has his own clothing range?

14. Theophilus was the middle name of which West Indian quick who spent a decade playing for Surrey?

15. Which Indian took the most wickets by a pace bowler in Test matches in 2011?

16. Who holds the record for the most ten-wicket match hauls in Tests by a West Indian bowler?

17. Who dismissed Alastair Cook in August 2008 to claim his 350th Test victim?

18. Which former javelin thrower took 7 for 81 on his Test debut for South Africa against Sri Lanka in December 2011?

19. Which fearsome West Indian fast bowler is also a qualified commercial airline pilot?
    a) Colin Croft
    b) Kenny Benjamin
    c) Michael Holding

20. Which bowler has the best Test strike rate?
    a) Shane Bond
    b) Malcolm Marshall
    c) Waqar Younis

Answers to Quiz 56: Pot Luck

1. Ian Bell
2. 1970s
3. Jack Bannister
4. Richie Richardson
5. Graham Gooch
6. Robin Smith
7. Somerset
8. Glamorgan, Hampshire and Worcestershire
9. Warwickshire and Worcestershire
10. Tim Bresnan
11. Kabir Ali
12. 291
13. Sreesanth
14. India
15. Delhi Daredevils
16. Stuart Broad (his sister is Gemma)
17. Garfield Sobers
18. Australia, West Indies and World XI
19. Fred Trueman
20. AC Milan

MEDIUM

Quiz 58: Pot Luck

1. Who took more Test wickets for Australia – Merv Hughes or Geoff Lawson?

2. What is the name of the club that is open to anyone who has ever made a first ball duck?

3. The Sinhalese Sports Club Ground is a Test venue in which city?

4. How are Shaun and Graeme Pollock related?

5. Which fielder has taken the most catches in Test cricket history?

6. What happened in England's 2003 Test against Sri Lanka in Galle that hasn't occurred since?

7. Which bowler has dismissed Ricky Ponting the most times in Test cricket?

8. Who said after his first ever cage fight, 'I had more adrenaline out there in one night than I did in 17 years of cricket'?

9. Who holds the record for the fewest innings required to reach 2,000 first-class runs in a season?

10. The highest team total in a County Championship match in the 20th century was scored in 1990 by which county?

11. How many did they score?

12. Which England bowler took 9 for 37 in a County Championship match against Worcestershire in 2010?

13. Which England batsman scored 606 runs in four separate Cricket World Cups but never made a century?

14. Donald Bradman played domestic cricket for which two Australian states?

15. Who are the only country to successfully defend the ICC Trophy?

16. Which England Test batsman was a member of the England football squad for the 1950 football World Cup?

17. Which England batsman topped the batting averages of Division 2 of the County Championship in 2011?

18. Which Bangladeshi batsman scored a half century in just 27 minutes in a 2007 Test match against India?

19. How many times have England chased over 300 in the fourth innings to win a Test match?
    a) never
    b) twice
    c) 3 times

20. Which England batsman hit 10 sixes and 18 fours in an unbeaten 201 in a 2008 Friends Provident Trophy quarter final against Leicestershire?
    a) Ravi Bopara
    b) Kevin Pietersen
    c) Matt Prior

MEDIUM

Answers to Quiz 57: Pacemen

1. Curtly Ambrose
2. Northamptonshire
3. Shaun Tait
4. Harold Larwood
5. Jeff Thomson
6. Devon Malcolm
7. Dale Steyn
8. Kemar Roach
9. Lasith Malinga
10. Jason Gillespie
11. Fidel Edwards
12. Michael Clarke
13. Brett Lee
14. Sylvester Clarke
15. Ishant Sharma
16. Malcolm Marshall
17. Makyaha Ntini
18. Marchant de Lange
19. Colin Croft
20. Shane Bond

Quiz 59: Big-Hitters

1. Who hit 268 in a 50-over game for Surrey against Glamorgan in 2002?

2. Which West Indian tail ender smashed 25 off an Ian Botham over in a 1981 Test match?

3. Whose 69-ball century is the fastest in a One-Day International by an England batsman?

4. Which Australian holds the record for the most sixes in a first-class game with 20?

5. Which New Zealander smashed 16 sixes in an innings against Australia A in 2011?

6. Who hit a rapid-fire 86 from just 66 balls in the 1979 World Cup final?

7. Which Irishman scored the fastest century of the 2011 English domestic season?

8. Which all-rounder holds the record for the most sixes in a Test innings?

9. Kapil Dev hit four sixes from four balls to save the follow-on for India in a Test match against England in 1990. Who was the bowler?

10. In 1998, Andrew Flintoff hit 34 from an over from which England bowler?

11. Which West Indian clubbed 10 sixes while compiling a century against India in a 2011 ODI?

12. Which Somerset batsman hit more than fifty sixes in a season four times in the 1930s?

13. Allan Lamb scored 18 runs off the final over of a One-Day International to steer England to victory against Australia in 1986/87. Who was the unfortunate bowler?

14. Which New Zealander hit nine sixes in his 77 not out against England in Napier in 2008?

15. Two West Indians hit 13 sixes in Test matches in 2011. Dwayne Bravo was one, which all-rounder was the other?

16. Who was the first batsman to hit 100 Test match sixes?

17. Zulu was the nickname of which big-hitting all-rounder?

18. Which hard-hitting batsman was the first player to earn 100 Test caps for the West Indies?

19. Viv Richards hit the fastest Test century in history off how many balls?
    a) 56
    b) 57
    c) 58

20. Who has scored the most sixes for England in Test matches?
    a) Ian Botham
    b) Andrew Flintoff
    c) Kevin Pietersen

Answers to Quiz 58: Pot Luck

1. Merv Hughes
2. The Primary Club
3. Colombo
4. Nephew and uncle
5. Rahul Dravid
6. England fielded a Test XI made up completely of players born in England
7. Harbhajan Singh
8. Adam Hollioake
9. Mark Ramprakash
10. Lancashire
11. 863
12. Steve Finn
13. Alec Stewart
14. New South Wales and South Australia
15. Australia
16. Willie Watson
17. Andrew Strauss
18. Mohammad Ashraful
19. 3 times
20. Ravi Bopara

MEDIUM

Quiz 60: Pot Luck

1. What is the name of the feature on Test Match Special where guests from outside cricket are interviewed?

2. Who holds the record for the fastest Test match triple century?

3. Who played 71 ODIs for Australian between 1997 and 2004 but didn't win a Test cap?

4. In 2011, who became the first foreign coach of the Australian team?

5. Which Australian scored 151 on his Test debut against India in 2004?

6. Who captained Australia in two Twenty20 internationals against England after the 2010/11 Ashes series?

7. Shanthakumaran is the first name of which Indian bowler?

8. Which guitar-playing England batsman recorded the 2009 album Songs from the Sun House?

9. In what year did Nottinghamshire last win the County Championship?

10. Which Warwickshire captain was forced to apologise after saying that he 'would not go and watch a women's game unless they were wearing short skirts'?

11. Which wicket-keeper had seven dismissals in an innings in England's Test against India in 1980?

12. Who are the four West Indians to have taken 100 catches in Test cricket?

13. Who, in November 2011, became the second-youngest player to make his Test debut for Australia?

14. If every player in a team was out first ball, what number batsman would be not out at the end of the innings?

15. What was last used in England in 1939 and in Australia in 1979?

16. Who beat England in the final of the 2004 ICC Champions Trophy?

17. Which fielder has taken the most catches in Test matches for South Africa?

18. Which left-arm seamer was called up to the Indian Test team that faced England in 2011 after a three-year absence after Zaheer Khan was ruled out through injury?

19. Which team finished at the bottom of Division 2 in the 2011 County Championship?
   a) Essex
   b) Kent
   c) Leicestershire

20. Ricky Ponting recently set the record for the most Test catches by an Australian fielder. Who previously held the record?
   a) Mark Taylor
   b) Mark Waugh
   c) Steve Waugh

MEDIUM

Answers to Quiz 59: Big Hitters

1. Ali Brown
2. Andy Roberts
3. Kevin Pietersen
4. Andrew Symonds
5. Jesse Ryder
6. Collis King
7. Kevin O'Brien
8. Wasim Akram
9. Eddie Hemmings
10. Alex Tudor
11. Kieron Pollard
12. Arthur Wellard
13. Bruce Reid
14. Tim Southee
15. Darren Sammy
16. Adam Gilchrist
17. Lance Klusener
18. Clive Lloyd
19. 56
20. Andrew Flintoff

Quiz 61: Indian Premier League

1. In what year did the first IPL take place?

2. Who were the first winners of the competition?

3. Who captained the team to that maiden victory?

4. Which franchise did Virender Sehwag play for in the 2012 IPL?

5. Harbhajan Singh slapped which Indian international bowler during a match in 2008?

6. Which New Zealander scored a record-breaking 158 not out for Kolkata Knight Riders in 2008?

7. Which England batsman played for Rajasthan Royals in 2012?

8. Who were the three non-Indian franchise captains in the 2012 IPL?

9. Who were the first team to win the IPL twice?

10. Bought for $2m, which Indian all-rounder was the most expensive player sold in the 2012 IPL auction?

11. Which Indian veteran captained Rajasthan Royals in the 2012 competition?

12. Which England player was selected by Pune Warriors India for the 2012 competition?

13. Which Australian batsman was the coach of the Deccan Chargers in 2012?

14. Coming off just 37 balls for the Royals against Mumbai, which Indian holds the record for the fastest century in the history of the IPL?

15. Which Pakistani left-arm seamer took a record-breaking 6 for 14 for the Royals in 2008?

16. The Kings XI Punjab are based in which city?

17. With 8 wickets and 618 runs, who was named the 2011 Player of the Tournament?

18. Which franchise was added to the IPL in 2011 but lasted only one season?

19. Who was the first batsman to score two IPL centuries?
    a) Chris Gayle
    b) Adam Gilchrist
    c) Virender Sehwag

20. How many teams took part in the 2012 competition?
    a) 8
    b) 9
    c) 10

Answers to Quiz 60: Pot Luck

1. View From the Boundary
2. Virender Sehwag
3. Ian Harvey
4. Mickey Arthur
5. Michael Clarke
6. Cameron White
7. Sreesanth
8. Mark Butcher
9. 2005
10. Ian Westwood
11. Bob Taylor
12. Brian Lara, Viv Richards, Garfield Sobers and Carl Hooper
13. Pat Cummins
14. 8
15. 8 ball overs
16. West Indies
17. Jacques Kallis
18. RP Singh
19. Leicestershire
20. Mark Waugh

MEDIUM

Quiz 62: Pot Luck

1. What connects Hull City FC and the Bangladesh cricket team?

2. Who holds the record for the most dismissals in a Test match by an England wicket-keeper?

3. Which all-rounder took six wickets on his Test debut against England in 2002 but never played a Test for New Zealand again?

4. Who was Australia's leading wicket-taker in the 2010/11 Ashes series?

5. Irishmen William Porterfield and Boyd Rankin play English domestic cricket for which county?

6. Who was named ICC Umpire of the Year for the third time in a row in 2011?

7. Six After Six is the title of a book telling the story of which big-hitting batsman's 2011 World Cup?

8. Which Australian fast bowler who later coached Pakistan is a qualified optometrist?

9. Skid is the nickname of which former player-turned-writer and broadcaster?

10. What nationality is former Derbyshire seamer Ole Mortensen?

11. Alastair Cook, Simon Jones and Marcus Trescothick all share what birthday?

12. What happened on the second day of the 2000 Lord's Test that had never happened before?

13. Danish Kaneria played domestic cricket in England for which county?

14. Who is the only player to score Test centuries for two different countries?

15. Which batsman played 51 ODIs for England in between 2000 and 2006 but never won a Test cap?

Answers – page 129

16. Who played 71 Tests for England between 1997 and 2004 but never played a One-Day International?

17. Which former Australian Test batsman has a black belt in taekwondo?

18. Northlands Road was the former home of which county?

19. Which cricket-inspired band had a 2012 number 1 hit with Twilight?
    a) Cover Drive
    b) Late Cut
    c) Second Slip

20. What is the record for the most consecutive Test victories by England?
    a) 7
    b) 8
    c) 9

Answers to Quiz 61: Indian Premier League

1. 2008
2. Rajasthan Royals
3. Shane Warne
4. Delhi Daredevils
5. Sreesanth
6. Brendon McCullum
7. Owais Shah
8. Kumar Sangakkara, Daniel Vettori and Adam Gilchrist
9. Chennai Super Kings
10. Ravindra Jadeja
11. Rahul Dravid
12. Luke Wright
13. Darren Lehmann
14. Yusuf Pathan
15. Sohail Tanvir
16. Chandigarh
17. Chris Gayle
18. Kochi Tuskers Kerala
19. Chris Gayle
20. 9

Quiz 63: Wicket-Keepers

1. Which Australian-born keeper played 11 Tests for England in 2008/09?

2. Who came out as cricket's first openly gay cricketer in 2011?

3. Which former England stumper wore the same hat throughout his career?

4. Which New Zealand wicket-keeper's 173 against Pakistan in 1990 is the highest Test score by a number nine batsman?

5. Who holds the record for the highest score by a wicket-keeper in a One-Day International?

6. Who is the only England wicket-keeper to score a century and bag five dismissals in an innings in the same Test match?

7. Which Australian made his maiden Test century against the West Indies in 2012?

8. Which former England wicket-keeper is the coach of the Belgium under 16 rugby team?

9. Who are the two Pakistani wicket-keepers with 200 Test dismissals to their name?

10. Which wicket-keeper has scored nine Test match double centuries?

11. Which former South Africa keeper, whose son now plays for Durham, was named the ICC's first General Manager?

12. Chucky was the nickname of which England wicket-keeper?

13. Which climbing-loving England gloveman was given a leave of absence on a tour to India so he could visit Mount Everest?

14. Which former England keeper was banned by the ECB for two matches in 2011 for persistent misconduct of Essex players under his leadership?

15. Which England keeper had never been dismissed for a duck in his Test career before bagging a pair in his final two innings?

16. Jeffrey Dujon is one of two West Indian wicket-keepers with 200 Test dismissals. Who is the other?

17. Which wicket-keeper scored the fastest Test century of 2011?

18. Which English wicket-keeper has the most Test dismissals?
    a) Alan Knott
    b) Jack Russell
    c) Alec Stewart

19. Who holds the record for the most dismissals in Test cricket?
    a) Mark Boucher
    b) Adam Gilchrist
    c) Ian Healy

MEDIUM

Answers to Quiz 62: Pot Luck

1. They're both nicknamed The Tigers
2. Jack Russell
3. Andre Adams
4. Mitchell Johnson
5. Warwickshire
6. Aleem Dar
7. Kevin O'Brien
8. Geoff Lawson
9. Vic Marks
10. Danish
11. 25 December
12. All four innings took place on the same day
13. Essex
14. Kepler Wessels
15. Vikram Solanki
16. Mark Butcher
17. Justin Langer
18. Hampshire
19. Cover Drive
20. 8

Quiz 64: Pot Luck

1. Excluding England and Australia, which side has played the most Test matches?

2. Who, in 2002, set the record for the most Test runs by an English batsman in a calendar year?

3. Who was the first batsman to score 8,000 Test match runs?

4. Who scored 123 out of Australia's second innings total of 184 against England in 1999?

5. Alastair Cook's career-best innings of 294 was scored against which opposition?

6. Which West Indian holds the record for the highest Test innings by a number 11 batsman?

7. Which all-rounder played 14 ODIs for England in 2004 and 2005 and was added to the reserve umpire panel in 2011?

8. Which two players opened the bowling for England in the 2010 World Twenty20 final?

9. Which Australian got spooked during a stay at the supposedly haunted Lumley Castle Hotel and ended up taking sanctuary on Brett Lee's floor?

10. Goober is the nickname of which current England international?

11. Which diminutive wicket-keeper succeeded Jeffrey Dujon in the West Indies side, making seven ducks in 18 completed Test innings?

12. Which West Indian quickie said to David Boon, 'Now David, are you going to get out now or am I going to have to bowl around the wicket and kill you?'?

13. Which England international's doorbell plays the Blaydon Races, in honour of his love for Newcastle United?

14. Can you name the two players to have scored two Test match triple hundreds and taken a Test match five for?

15. The M. Chinnaswamy Stadium is in which Indian city?

16. Former England captain Michael Vaughan was born in which city?

17. Which West Indian Test player's first name is the same as the surname of an eight-time tennis Grand Slam tournament winner?

18. Which Pakistani was given a one Test and two ODI ban for deliberately roughing up the pitch in a 2005 Test against England?

19. Adam Gilchrist had a brief spell in England with which county?
    a) Kent
    b) Middlesex
    c) Surrey

20. Which batsman smashed 13 sixes in an innings of 128 not out against the Daredevils in 2012?
    a) Chris Gayle
    b) Brendon McCullum
    c) Andrew Symonds

MEDIUM

Answers to Quiz 63: Wicket-Keepers

1. Tim Ambrose
2. Steven Davies
3. Jack Russell
4. Ian Smith
5. Mahendra Singh Dhoni
6. Matt Prior
7. Matthew Wade
8. Jack Richards
9. Wasim Bari and Kamran Akmal
10. Kumar Sangakkara
11. Dave Richardson
12. Warren Hegg
13. Bruce French
14. James Foster
15. Geraint Jones
16. Ridley Jacobs
17. Matt Prior
18. Alan Knott
19. Mark Boucher

Quiz 65: England

1. Devon Malcolm famously took 9 for 57 against South Africa in 1994. Which England bowler took the other wicket?

2. Which South African scored 94 in that innings and wasn't dismissed by Malcolm?

3. Four of England's five bowlers in that match were born outside England. Devon Malcolm was one, who were the other three?

4. Which batsman captained the England Lions in their 2012 game against the West Indies?

5. Who took 7 for 109 for England in the 2006/07 Ashes Test in Adelaide?

6. Which England selector won his only Test cap on England's victorious 1986/87 Ashes tour?

7. Why was England's timeless Test against South Africa in 1939 cut short?

8. How many ODI centuries did Ian Botham score?

9. Which batsman played 88 ODIs for England between 1989 and 2003 but never won a Man of the Match award?

10. What do Archie MacLaren, Allan Lamb, Andrew Strauss, Kevin Pietersen and most recently Alastair Cook all have in common?

11. Who is the only person to play Test cricket for both England and India?

12. Who holds the record for the most Test match not outs by an England batsman?

13. Who captained England on their 2005/06 Test tour to India?

14. Which pair of Sky commentators hold the record for England's highest tenth-wicket Test partnership against India?

15. Who holds the record for the most Test defeats as England captain?

Answers – page 135

16. Who is the oldest player to play for England in a T20 international?

17. Who is the only England batsman with a career Test match batting average of over 60?

18. Which England bowler, who shares his name with a character from children's TV, was the first man to take 100 Test wickets?

19. Who has scored the most Test runs for England without scoring a century?
    a) Mike Brearley
    b) John Emburey
    c) Ashley Giles

20. Who scored the most Test centuries out of
    a) Paul Collingwood
    b) Mike Gatting
    c) Robin Smith

Answers to Quiz 64: Pot Luck

1. West Indies
2. Michael Vaughan
3. Garfield Sobers
4. Michael Slater
5. India
6. Tino Best
7. Alex Wharf
8. Ryan Sidebottom and Tim Bresnan
9. Shane Watson
10. Chris Tremlett
11. David Williams
12. Malcolm Marshall
13. Graeme Swann
14. Chris Gayle and Virender Sehwag
15. Bangalore
16. Manchester
17. Lendl Simmons
18. Shahid Afridi
19. Middlesex
20. Chris Gayle

MEDIUM

Quiz 66: Pot Luck

1. Which Australian scored over 3,000 Test runs, including 12 half-centuries but never reached three figures?

2. Which two Test teams compete for the Wisden Trophy?

3. Which county won the first two Gillette Cup competitions?

4. Which West Indian was England's bowling coach from 2007 to 2010?

5. Brian Johnston famously lost it on air after which player 'didn't quite get his leg over'?

6. Elias Bunny was named man of the match on his 2011 Test debut. Which country does he play for?

7. Which Australian left-armer scored his first ODI run in his 20th game?

8. Who is the only bowler to take 10 wickets in a match against all nine other Test-playing nations?

9. Who was the first player to take part in 100 Test victories?

10. In 2003, which England seamer became the first player to take two wickets in his first over in Test match cricket?

11. In which country will you find teams called Aces, Wizards, Stags, Knights, Volts and Firebirds?

12. Monty Panesar scored his highest Test score of 16 against which country?

13. Who was the first player to score a century in a Cricket World Cup final?

14. The film Out of the Ashes is about which country's cricket team?

15. Who, in 2010, became the only number 8 batsman to hit back-to-back Test hundreds?

16. After retiring from the game, which cricketer became a representative to the United Nations for Trinidad and Tobago?

17. The trophy awarded to the winner of the ICC World Player of the Year is named after which player?

18. Who was the only specialist wicket-keeper in England's 2007 Cricket World Cup squad?

19. Who was the leading Test run-scorer of the 2000s?
    a) Rahul Dravid
    b) Ricky Ponting
    c) Sachin Tendulkar

20. What is the middle name of West Indian opener Adrian Barath?
    a) Boris
    b) Brian
    c) Ken

Answers to Quiz 65: England

1. Darren Gough
2. Daryll Cullinan
3. Phil DeFreitas, Joey Benjamin and Graeme Hick
4. James Taylor
5. Matthew Hoggard
6. James Whitaker
7. The England team had to catch a boat home
8. None
9. Nasser Hussain
10. They scored a century in their first Test match as captain of England

11. The Nawab of Pataudi senior
12. Bob Willis
13. Andrew Flintoff
14. Paul Allott and Bob Willis
15. Michael Atherton
16. Paul Nixon
17. Herbert Sutcliffe
18. Johnny Briggs
19. John Emburey
20. Paul Collingwood

MEDIUM

Quiz 67: Anagrams

Find the player from the following anagrams:

1. A Brats Tudor

2. Swaddled Fire

3. Lavender Horn Nip

4. Handmade Hiring Nosh

5. Red Jerseys

6. Achy Hue Smiles

7. Smelly Ilk

8. Koala Orca Tis

9. A Heartland Tails Link

10. Marine Goon

11. Manager News

12. A Sealed Jam

13. Alias Tempt

14. Add Hard Bin

15. Racy Sleigh

16. Headland Roar Fin

17. Aha Monsignor

18. Bras Men Nit

19. Raja Send Omens

20. Lean Fat Ump

MEDIUM

Answers to Quiz 66: Pot Luck

1. Shane Warne
2. England and the West Indies
3. Sussex
4. Ottis Gibson
5. Ian Botham
6. Bangladesh
7. Doug Bollinger
8. Muttiah Muralitharan
9. Ricky Ponting
10. Richard Johnson
11. New Zealand
12. Sri Lanka
13. Clive Lloyd
14. Afghanistan
15. Harbhajan Singh
16. Deryck Murray
17. Garfield Sobers
18. Paul Nixon
19. Ricky Ponting
20. Boris

DIFFICULT QUIZZES

Quiz 68: Pot Luck

1. Which 20th-century British Prime Minister played first-class cricket?

2. Which American singer performed at the opening of the 2012 Indian Premier League?

3. England internationals Bob Woolmer and Robin Jackman were born in which country?

4. What was Gubby Allen's real first name?

5. Which Australian wicket-keeper won his only Test cap against England at Edgbaston in 2009?

6. Which bowler / wicket-keeper pairing has combined to take the most wickets in One-Day International history?

7. Who are the four West Indians to have scored a Test century in under 75 balls?

8. Which Australian batted on all five days of a Test match in 1980 and hit a six on each and every day?

9. Which two countries took part in the first official international cricket match?

10. Which England player was dismissed for a duck in five out of seven innings in the 1998/99 Ashes?

11. Bangladesh beat Australia in a 2005 One-Day International at which British ground?

12. In 2001, which batsman became only the second Englishman to be dismissed handled the ball in a Test match?

13. Which Warwickshire all-rounder was named the Professional Cricketers' Association Player of the Year for 2010?

14. Who holds the record for the most Test match caught and bowled dismissals by an English bowler?

15. Which England bowler was denied a Test hat trick against Bangladesh in 2005 when the ball hit the middle stump but didn't dislodge the bails?

16. Who is the only Pakistani to have scored a century before lunch on the opening day of a Test match?

17. Essex provided four players for the England team for the first time in 1988. Name the quartet.

18. Ian, Greg and Trevor Chappell are the grandsons of which Australian Test player?

19. Which international team played Test cricket first?
    a) India
    b) New Zealand
    c) West Indies

20. In what year was the MCC formed?
    a) 1787
    b) 1877
    c) 1887

Answers to Quiz 100: Pot Luck

1. Bert Ironmonger, Jack Iverson and John Inverarity
2. Tony Lewis
3. Ross Taylor
4. Shahid Afridi and Abdul Razzaq
5. Geoff Allott
6. Brad Hodge
7. Worcestershire
8. Ivan
9. Jamie Dalrymple
10. Ryan Sidebottom
11. Jeremy Snape
12. Steve Finn
13. Jack Richards
14. Ajmal Shahzad
15. Daniel Christian
16. Matthew Hoggard
17. Vasbert Drakes
18. Altrincham FC
19. Allan Lamb
20. 98

DIFFICULT

Quiz 69: The Ashes

1. Which Australian bagged a king pair in the 2010 Brisbane Test?

2. Which Englishman took his second and third Ashes wickets on the 2010/11 tour?

3. Gary Pratt famously ran out Ricky Ponting at Trent Bridge in 2005 but which other sub, now a prolific Somerset batsman, caught him out at Lord's?

4. The most runs conceded in a single Ashes over is 24. Who was the unfortunate bowler?

5. Taking some 326 balls, which opening batsmen scored the slowest century in Ashes history?

6. Which England batsman averaged 39.78 in 15 Ashes Tests between 1989 and 1993 but was never on a winning team?

7. In what year did Australia last fail to win a single Test in an Ashes series?

8. Which Australian was out hit wicket in the second innings of the amazing 2005 Test at Edgbaston?

9. Which football ground staged its one and only Ashes Test in 1902?

10. Who captained England in the first ever Ashes Test match?

11. Which Australian bowler badly damaged his shoulder attempting to rugby-tackle a drunken pitch invader in 1982?

12. The Sydney Test in 1970/71 was disrupted after which tailender was felled by a John Snow bouncer?

13. Which Australian bowler took 20 wickets at an average of 33.5 in six matches between 1997 and 2005 but was never on the winning side?

14. Which two batsmen, one English and one Australian, were dismissed on 99 at Lord's in 1993?

15. Who was the Daily Mirror's Mike Walters describing when he wrote, 'With the possible exception of Rolf Harris, no other Australian has inflicted more pain and grief on Englishmen since Don Bradman'?

16. Which Australian opening pair closed the opening day of the 1989 Trent Bridge Test unbeaten on 310-0?

17. Bob Willis took 8 wickets in the second innings of England's Ashes win at Headingley in 1981, but who took the other two wickets?

18. England fielded 29 players in the disastrous 1989 series. Who were the only two players to play in all six Tests?

19. Prior to 2009, when was the last time that England beat Australia in a Lord's Test?
    a) 1934
    b) 1938
    c) 1953

20. Who compiled the most ducks in Ashes matches?
    a) Darren Gough
    b) Glenn McGrath
    c) Phil Tufnell

Answers to Quiz 68: Pot Luck

1. Alec Douglas-Home
2. Katy Perry
3. India
4. George
5. Graham Manou
6. Makhaya Ntini and Mark Boucher
7. Viv Richards, Shivnarine Chanderpaul, Chris Gayle and Roy Fredericks
8. Kim Hughes
9. Canada and the USA
10. Alan Mullally
11. Cardiff's Sophia Gardens
12. Michael Vaughan
13. Neil Carter
14. Derek Underwood
15. Chris Tremlett
16. Majid Khan
17. Graham Gooch, Derek Pringle, John Childs and Neil Foster
18. Vic Richardson
19. West Indies
20. 1787

DIFFICULT

Quiz 70: Pot Luck

1. Which cricketer won the first Twitter libel case?

2. The Guardian's Frank Keating likened which fast bowler's run-up to 'a 1914 biplane tied up with elastic bands trying vainly to take off'?

3. Which two Australian left-arm spinners made their Test debut in the 2010/11 Ashes series?

4. Which Hollywood star played Douglas Jardine in the TV series Bodyline?

5. The Rolling Stones' Charlie Watts would sign into hotels using which cricket commentator's name as a pseudonym?

6. Which Australian was the first batsman to wear a helmet in a Test match?

7. The trophy awarded to the winners of Test series between England and South Africa is named after which player?

8. What did Albert Trott do in 1899 that no man has since managed?

9. Who took 2,218 wickets at 22.32 in his county career but was never picked for England?

10. Who are the only two first-class counties that never won the Gillette Cup in any of its various incarnations?

11. What surname links a West Indian fast bowler who played five Tests between 1993 and 1994 and an Aussie who took six wickets on his Test debut in 2011?

12. Which Warwickshire batsman scored two County Championship double centuries in 2011?

13. What does the A in AB de Villiers stand for?

14. Which England batsman scored a hundred before lunch in a Test match against Bangladesh in 2005?

15. Who bowled a beamer, albeit with a tennis ball, at US President George W Bush who was on a visit to Pakistan in 2006?

16. In which city did Pakistan play their first home Test match?

17. Which England batsman went 119 innings without being dismissed for a duck between 1982 and 1990?

18. Which batsman holds the record for the most Test centuries in a calendar year?

19. The brother of which British politician represented Mohammad Asif at the ICC match-fixing tribunal?
    a) David Cameron
    b) Nick Clegg
    c) George Osborne

20. Which team scored 411 for 8 in a 2009 ODI and still lost the match?
    a) England
    b) South Africa
    c) Sri Lanka

Answers to Quiz 69: The Ashes

1. Ryan Harris
2. Paul Collingwood
3. James Hildreth
4. Monty Panesar at the hands of Adam Gilchrist in 2006/07
5. Michael Atherton
6. Robin Smith
7. 1977
8. Shane Warne
9. Bramall Lane
10. James Lillywhite Jr
11. Terry Alderman
12. Terry Jenner
13. Michael Kasprowicz
14. Michael Atherton and Mark Waugh
15. Steve Waugh
16. Mark Taylor and Geoff Marsh
17. Ian Botham and Chris Old with one apiece
18. David Gower and Jack Russell
19. 1934
20. Glenn McGrath

DIFFICULT

Quiz 71: What's in a Name?

1. Which former England opening batsman's middle name is Orlando?

2. Cuthbert is the real first name of which prolific former West Indian batsman who made his Test debut in 1974?

3. Which England all-rounder was named after the scorer of the winning goal in the 1981 FA Cup Final?

4. Shrek was the nickname of which leading England bowler?

5. Dalenano is the middle name of which Sussex, Warwickshire, Middlesex and West Indies seam bowler?

6. Which Australian all-rounder has the same name as a notorious American serial killer?

7. Which Kent seamer is nicknamed Ogre?

8. Verdon is the middle name of which South African Test veteran?

9. What is the New Zealand equivalent of the Barmy Army?

10. Gunner is the nickname of which international umpire?

11. Who did Shane Warne christen The Shermanator after a character from the film American Pie?

12. Which Aussie was nicknamed Fruitfly (the biggest Australian pest!)?

13. Which current England international's nickname is Cheese?

14. Edward Killeen are the middle names of which Australian batsman?

15. Which Middlesex seamer is nicknamed Dial M?

16. Skull is the nickname of which Australian spinner-turned-pundit?

17. Which feisty former Australian batsman's middle name is Clarence?

18. Which trio of New Zealand medium pacers at the 1992 World Cup were nicknamed Dibbly, Dobbly and Wobbly?

19. Chaminda Vaas's initials are WPUJC. What does the J stand for?
a) James
b) John
c) Joseph

20. Henderson is the middle name of which West Indian?
a) Chris Gayle
b) Darren Sammy
c) Fidel Edwards

Answers to Quiz 70: Pot Luck

1. Chris Cairns
2. Bob Willis
3. Xavier Doherty and Michael Beer
4. Hugo Weaving
5. Peter West
6. Graham Yallop
7. Basil D'Oliveira
8. He hit a six over the Lord's pavilion
9. Glamorgan's Don Shepherd
10. Glamorgan and Leicestershire
11. Cummins (Anderson and Pat)
12. Varun Chopra
13. Abraham
14. Ian Bell
15. Inzamam ul Haq
16. Dhaka (which is now in Bangladesh)
17. David Gower
18. Mohammad Yousuf
19. David Cameron (his brother, Alexander, is a barrister)
20. Sri Lanka

DIFFICULT

Quiz 72: Pot Luck

1. The Vulture Street End and The Stanley Street End are features of which Test venue?

2. England fielded seven foreign-born players in a 1992 Test match against New Zealand. Can you name them?

3. Which Australian was reprimanded by the match referee for damaging a TV after being run out in a 2011 World Cup game against Zimbabwe?

4. At which country ground will you find the Nackington Road End?

5. Which England captain was given the original Ashes urn?

6. Who captained the Rest of the World side that took on England and Australia in 1970/71?

7. Which Aussie spinner was dismissed for a duck in five consecutive Test match innings in 1985?

8. Who is England's leading scorer in One-Day Internationals against Australia?

9. Which commentator famously described New Zealander Bob Cunis as being 'neither one thing nor the other'?

10. The Chinaman delivery is named after which Trinidadian spinner?

11. What was special about Sam Kelsall and Karl Turner opening the batting in Nottinghamshire's County Championship match against Durham in 2011?

12. Since two divisions were introduced in 2000, which Essex bowler holds the record for the most County Championship wickets in a season?

13. Who is the only batsman to be dismissed for obstructing the field in a Test match?

14. Which Gloucestershire all-rounder in 2011 became the first English-born player to score 1,000 runs and take 50 wickets in his maiden County Championship season?

15. Which England batsman was the first to score 1,000 first-class runs in the 2011 season?

16. What was the name of the cricket-inspired 2003 film starring Delroy Lindo?

17. Who holds the record for the most international runs (Tests, ODIs and T20s) by an England batsman in a calendar year?

18. Who was withdrawn from the Pakistan attack in their 2003 World Cup match against Australia after bowling two beamers at Andrew Symonds?

19. How long did New Zealand have to wait from their Test debut to claim their first series win?
    a) 14 years
    b) 24 years
    c) 40 years

20. What caused a delay in the Sri Lanka v England Test in Kandy in 2007?
    a) a swarm of bees hovered over the wicket
    b) a snake slithered on to the pitch
    c) a fielder was bitten by a dog

Answers to Quiz 71: What's in a Name?

1. Roland Butcher
2. Gordon Greenidge
3. Rikki Clarke
4. Matthew Hoggard
5. Corey Collymore
6. Gary Gilmour
7. Charlie Shreck
8. Mark Boucher
9. The Beige Brigade
10. Ian Gould
11. Ian Bell

12. Merv Hughes
13. Matt Prior
14. Michael Hussey
15. Tim Murtagh
16. Kerry O'Keefe
17. David Boon
18. Gavin Larsen, Chris Harris and Rod Latham
19. Joseph
20. Fidel Edwards

DIFFICULT

Quiz 73: Cricket World Cup

1. Australia beat India in the 1987 and 1992 World Cups. What was the margin of victory in both matches?

2. Who are the two players to have played in Cricket World Cups for different countries?

3. Up to and including the 2011 competition, Australia had won the most matches. Who have won the second-largest number of matches?

4. In addition to 362 runs and 15 wickets, which Indian took four Man of the Match awards in 2011?

5. Which West Indian took 7-51 in a 1983 win over Australia?

6. Australia famously beat South Africa in the 1999 semifinal at which ground?

7. Who has recorded the highest individual score for England in a World Cup match?

8. Which two Australians have scored three centuries in a single World Cup tournament?

9. Which Englishman scored half-centuries in four consecutive matches at the 1983 World Cup?

10. Ireland beat which two countries at the 2011 World Cup?

11. Tim Bresnan is one of two Englishmen to have taken 5 wickets in a World Cup match for England. Which spinner is the other?

12. India notched up the highest score in World Cup history in 2007 by making 413-5 against which country?

13. Who holds the record for the most World Cup appearances?

14. Which Indian seamer took the first World Cup hat trick against New Zealand in 1983?

15. Who scored 119 for the Netherlands in their 2011 group game against England?

16. The highest ever World Cup innings of 188 not out was scored by which batsman?

17. Which country has compiled the two lowest scores in the World Cup history?

18. Up to 2011, which ground had hosted the most World Cup matches?

19. New Zealand's Brendon McCullum scored the fastest fifty in World Cup history. How many balls did it take him?
    a) 19
    b) 20
    c) 21

20. The oldest player to appear in the Cricket World Cup was 47-year-old Nolan Clarke. What country did he represent?
    a) Canada
    b) Kenya
    c) Netherlands

Answers to Quiz 72: Pot Luck

1. The Gabba
2. Graeme Hick, Alan Lamb, Robin Smith, Dermot Reeve, Derek Pringle, Chris Lewis and Philip Defreitas
3. Ricky Ponting
4. St Lawrence Ground, Canterbury
5. Ivo Bligh
6. Garfield Sobers
7. Bob Holland
8. Graham Gooch
9. John Arlott
10. Ellis 'Puss' Achong
11. They were both making their first-class debut
12. David Masters
13. Len Hutton
14. Will Gidman
15. Alastair Cook
16. Wondrous Oblivion
17. Kevin Pietersen
18. Waqar Younis
19. 40 years
20. A swarm of bees hovered over the wicket

DIFFICULT

Quiz 74: Pot Luck

1. Which Australian fast bowler's real surname was Durtanovich?

2. What is the name of the trophy awarded to the winners of Test series between England and India?

3. Who holds the record for the most expensive bowling figures in a One-Day International for England?

4. In what country do teams compete for the Logan Cup?

5. Which Sussex batsman played 44 games for Brighton and Hove Albion?

6. Who are the four batsmen to have scored more than one Test match triple century?

7. Cricket was a medal event at the 1998 Commonwealth Games. Which team took gold?

8. Which country will host the World Twenty20 in 2014?

9. Which England bowler was called for throwing in a Test match in 1986?

10. Who succeeded Scyld Berry as the editor of the 2012 Wisden Cricketers' Almanack?

11. Which fast bowler has competed in Alpine skiing World Cup competitions?

12. Who holds the record for bagging the most pairs in Test cricket?

13. Who scored his first century in his 150th Test innings against England in 2007?

14. Which Australian scored a century in his Test debut in 1970 and in his last Test appearance in 1984?

15. With 1,567 runs, which left-handers are England's most prolific ODI opening partnership?

16. What is Monty Panesar's real first name?

17. The Marrara Stadium is a Test venue in which Australian city?

18. How did Michael Angelow make history at Lord's in 1975?

19. What was prolific batsman Patsy Hendren's real first name?
    a) Elias
    b) Enoch
    c) Ebeneezer

20. In what year did Bangladesh make their Test debut?
    a) 1999
    b) 2000
    c) 2001

Answers to Quiz 73: Cricket World Cup

1. 1 run
2. Kepler Wessels and Anderson Cummins
3. New Zealand with 40
4. Yuvraj Singh
5. Winston Davis
6. Edgbaston
7. Andrew Strauss with 158 against India in 2011
8. Mark Waugh and Matthew Hayden
9. Graeme Fowler
10. England and the Netherlands
11. Vic Marks
12. Bermuda
13. Ricky Ponting with 46
14. Chetan Sharma
15. Ryan ten Doeschate
16. Gary Kirsten
17. Canada
18. Headingley
19. 20
20. Netherlands

DIFFICULT

Quiz 75: Left-handed Batsmen

1. Who holds the record for the highest Test score at the Gabba?

2. Which left-hander made his England debut against Bangladesh in 2010?

3. Which England opener was struck by a Malcolm Marshall bouncer in 1984 and never played Test cricket again?

4. Which West Indian underwent heart surgery after retiring hurt against Australia in 2005?

5. Who, in 2008, became the first white player to play for the West Indies since Geoff Greenidge?

6. Which southpaw captained the Rest of the World team that took on Australia in 2005?

7. Which England batsman scored a Test century against Pakistan in 2000 that contained just one boundary?

8. Which opener scored 67 on his maiden ODI appearance and played eight more games for England in 2009?

9. Who was named Wisden's Leading Cricketer in the World for 2011?

10. Which South African scored an unbeaten 222 on his Test debut against Bangladesh in 2003?

11. Which West Indian scored his maiden Test century against Bangladesh in October 2011?

12. In 109 ODIs between 1983 and 1994 which gritty left-hander was never dismissed for a duck?

13. Which West Indian batsman was reinstated after being controversially run out by Tony Greig in Trinidad in 1974?

14. Who holds the record for the most ducks in ODI history with 34?

15. Which left-hander scored his only ODI century for England against Australia in 2007?

Answers – page 157

16. Who scored 2,092 ODI runs for England in 71 innings for England between 1987 and 1999?

17. Which Aussie has had spells at Derbyshire, Durham, Gloucestershire, Hampshire and Lancashire?

18. True or false – David Gower's career Test average never dropped below 40?

19. Who scored 275 for South Africa against England in 1999?
    a) Gary Kirsten
    b) Graham Smith
    c) Lance Klusener

20. Which left-hander had the best Test match average out of
    a) Graham Thorpe
    b) Marcus Trescothick
    c) David Gower

Answers to Quiz 74: Pot Luck

1. Len Pascoe
2. The Pataudi Trophy
3. Steve Harmison 0-97 against Sri Lanka in 2006
4. Zimbabwe
5. Joe Gatting
6. Don Bradman, Brian Lara, Virender Sehwag and Chris Gayle
7. South Africa
8. Bangladesh
9. David Gower
10. Lawrence Booth
11. Dirk Nannes
12. Chris Martin
13. Anil Kumble
14. Greg Chappell
15. Trescothick and Knight
16. Mudhsuden
17. Darwin
18. He was the first streaker at a Test match in England
19. Elias
20. 1999

DIFFICULT

Quiz 76: Pot Luck

1. Who are the six batsmen to have scored a century in a World Cup final?

2. In 1930, Andy Sandham became the first man to do what in a Test match?

3. Which woman was named as one of Wisden's five cricketers of the year in 2009?

4. Which New Zealand opener is missing two toes after a childhood accident involving a fork-lift truck?

5. Which Warwickshire all-rounder, who played three Tests for England, plays in a band called Too Tone Deaf?

6. Who is the oldest post-war batsman to score a Test century at Lord's?

7. How many Test centuries did Sachin Tendulkar score at Lord's?

8. Who are the three non-Asian players to have taken ten wickets in a Test match in Asia on more than one occasion?

9. Which former England captain was appointed a tourism ambassador for Sri Lanka in 2012?

10. Who is the only England batsman to score over 150 in three ODIs?

11. Which West Indian, in 1972, became the first man to score a century in both innings on his Test debut?

12. Which former England seam bowler went on to become a pundit on the Sky Poker TV channel?

13. Which Australian fast bowler scored just 93 runs in 27 Test matches for Australia between 1985 and 1992?

14. Only once have both England openers scored a century in the same ODI. Who were the two batsmen?

15. With 60 dismissals, what is England's most successful Test bowler wicket-keeper combination?

Answers – page 159

16. Who is the only batsman to score a Test century in his first innings against each of his first three opponents?

17. England seamer Graham Onions is a fan of which football club?

18. Which five players made their Test debut for England in 2010?

19. Shahid Afridi holds the record for the fastest One-Day International century. How many balls did it take him?
    a) 37
    b) 38
    c) 39

20. How old was Afridi when he scored the fastest hundred?
    a) 16
    b) 17
    c) 18

Answers to Quiz 75: Left-handed Batsmen

1. Alastair Cook
2. Michael Carberry
3. Andy Lloyd
4. Chris Gayle
5. Brendan Nash
6. Graeme Smith
7. Graham Thorpe
8. Joe Denly
9. Kumar Sangakkara
10. Jacques Rudolph
11. Darren Bravo
12. Kepler Wessels
13. Alvin Kallicharran
14. Sanath Jayasuriya
15. Ed Joyce
16. Neil Fairbrother
17. Marcus North
18. True
19. Gary Kirsten
20. Graham Thorpe

DIFFICULT

Quiz 77: Spinners part 1

1. Which alliterative spinner in 2012 became the fifth player from Dominica to play Test cricket for the West Indies?

2. Which England spinner made his Test debut in the same match that Shane Warne delivered 'The Ball of the Century'?

3. Who was bowling when Brian Lara scored his record-breaking 400th run against England in Antigua in 2004?

4. Which Australian spinner was the first man to take 200 Test wickets?

5. Which Indian batsman did Monty Panesar dismiss to claim his maiden Test wicket?

6. Who took 4-48 in England's 2011 World Cup win over the West Indies in 2011?

7. Which English off-spinner took 414 first-class wickets for Northants and Notts between 1996 and 2009 but never played a game for England?

8. The best ever first-class bowling figures of 10-10 were recorded by which Yorkshire spinner?

9. Which 41-year-old twirler, who was coaching in Papua New Guinea, was recalled to the Australian T20 team in 2012?

10. Who holds the record for the most Test wickets taken by a Pakistani spinner?

11. Of bowlers to have take at least 100 Test wickets, who has the highest average?

12. Which spinner took four wickets for the West Indies when they dismissed England for just 51 in the 2009 Test in Jamaica?

13. Who is the only man to take nine wickets in a Test match innings for the West Indies?

14. Who took 30 wickets in Pakistan's three game Test series against England in 1987?

15. Which Australian took 12 wickets on his Test debut in 2008 but made only one more Test appearance?

16. Which West Indian was the fourth leading wicket-taker in Test cricket in 2011?

17. Who took 11 for 83 for England against Pakistan in 1984 but still ended up on the losing side?

18. Which South African went for 221 runs in 65 wicketless overs against Sri Lanka in 2006?

19. Who holds the record for the most ODI wickets in a calendar year?
    a) Anil Kumble
    b) Muttiah Muralitharan
    c) Saqlain Mushtaq

20. How old was Saeed Ajmal when he made his Test debut?
    a) 30
    b) 31
    c) 32

Answers to Quiz 76: Pot Luck

1. Clive Lloyd, Viv Richards, Aravinda de Silva, Ricky Ponting, Adam Gilchrist and Mahela Jayawardene
2. Score a triple century
3. Claire Taylor
4. Martin Guptill
5. Darren Maddy
6. Tom Graveney
7. None
8. Graeme Swann, Richard Hadlee and Shane Warne
9. Tony Greig
10. Andrew Strauss
11. Lawrence Rowe
12. Ed Giddins
13. Bruce Reid
14. Marcus Trescothick and Vikram Solanki
15. Ian Botham and Bob Taylor
16. Andrew Strauss
17. Newcastle United
18. Michael Carberry, Steve Finn, James Tredwell, Ajmal Shahzad and Eoin Morgan
19. 37
20. 16

DIFFICULT

Quiz 78: Pot Luck

1. Springbok Park is a cricket venue in which South African city?

2. Which former England captain was declared bankrupt after a hearing in Brisbane in July 2011?

3. What was the name of the former Essex bowler who was jailed in 2012 for spot-fixing?

4. Which former New Zealand wicket-keeper raised £50,000 for charity after reaching the summit of Mount Everest in 2011?

5. Which Middlesex tail-ender scored a century as a nightwatchman in a 2012 County Championship match against Nottinghamshire?

6. Which county coach is the brother of a former manager of Leeds United FC?

7. What do Trevor Bailey, Chris Balderstone, Ed Giddins and Devon Malcolm have in common?

8. Who holds the record for the most boundaries in a Test match innings?

9. The highest sixth-wicket partnership in Test cricket was set in 2009 by two players with the same surname. What was that surname?

10. Who is England's highest post-war run-scorer in Test matches against Australia?

11. Which Pakistani bowler's 43 against England at the 2003 World Cup is the highest ever ODI score by a number 11 batsman?

12. Who took 8 for 19 including a hat trick in a One-Day International against Zimbabwe in 2001/02?

13. Bing is the nickname of which Australian fast bowler?

14. Which Lancashire spinner took 9 for 51 in his side's 2011 County Championship win over Hampshire?

15. In 1987, who set (and still holds) the record for the most One-Day International wickets in a calendar year by an England bowler?

16. Who are the two South Africans to have scored centuries in three consecutive ODIs?

17. Which West Indian was on the winning side in his first ten Test appearances?

18. Which England batsman scored twice as many ODI runs in 2011 than his highest scoring teammate?

19. Which team were skittled for just 34 and 48 in County Championship matches in 2011?
    a) Derbyshire
    b) Leicestershire
    c) Northamptonshire

20. What freak weather conditions caused the abandonment of Pakistan's match against Zimbabwe in 1998?
    a) extreme heat
    b) fog
    c) continuous thunderstorms

Answers to Quiz 77: Spinners part 1

1. Shane Shillingford
2. Peter Such
3. Gareth Batty
4. Clarrie Grimmett
5. Sachin Tendulkar
6. James Tredwell
7. Jason Brown
8. Hedley Verity
9. Brad Hogg
10. Danish Kaneria
11. Carl Hooper
12. Sulieman Benn
13. Jack Noriega
14. Abdul Qadir
15. Jason Krejza
16. Devendra Bishoo
17. Nick Cook
18. Nicky Boje
19. Saqlain Mushtaq
20. 32

DIFFICULT

Quiz 79: All-Rounders

1. Which England all-rounder was fined half of his match fee on his Test debut in 2003?

2. Dwayne Bravo played in the Indian Premier League in 2012 for which team?

3. What do the initial CB in CB Fry stand for?

4. Who has won the most Test Player of the Match awards?

5. Which Leicestershire opening batsman took 4 for 22 in the 2011 Friends Life T20 final?

6. Which all-rounder did Mark Boucher dismiss to claim his only Test wicket?

7. Which England all-rounder didn't bat and took 0 for 43 from 9 overs in his only ODI against South Africa in 1996?

8. The father of which England all-rounder played for East Africa in the first ever Cricket World Cup?

9. Who took 4 for 10 in a Twenty20 match for England against the West Indies in September 2011?

10. Which West Indian all-rounder-turned-golfer is now the pro at the Sandy Lane resort in Barbados?

11. As well as playing for Warwickshire, Shaun Pollock spent a brief spell with which English county?

12. No Boundaries: Pain and Passion On and Off The Pitch is the title of the autobiography of which former England all-rounder?

13. Who scored his maiden Test century against England at Trent Bridge in 2012?

14. Who opened the batting and bowling for England in a Test match in Pakistan 1987?

15. Who was the last player with a double-barrelled surname to play Test cricket for England?

16. Which current West Indies all-rounder's favourite cricketer is Nasser Hussain?

17. Which Pakistani all-rounder scored a double century and took 5 for 49 in a 1973 Test match against New Zealand?

18. Who is the only Australian to score 100 runs and take ten wickets in the same Test match?

19. Who won six caps for the New Zealand ODI team in addition to 60 caps for the All Blacks rugby union team?
    a) Dan Carter
    b) Sean Fitzpatrick
    c) Jeff Wilson

20. Which South African was dismissed for 0 in the first innings and 99 in the second in the 2003 Headingley Test?
    a) Andrew Hall
    b) Brian McMillan
    c) Shaun Pollock

Answers to Quiz 78: Pot Luck

1. Bloemfontein
2. Adam Hollioake
3. Mervyn Westfield
4. Adam Parore
5. Ollie Rayner
6. Paul Grayson
7. They all bagged a pair in their final Test appearance
8. John Edrich with 52 fours and five sixes against New Zealand in 1965
9. Jayawardene
10. David Gower
11. Shoaib Akhtar
12. Chaminda Vaas
13. Brett Lee
14. Simon Kerrigan
15. John Emburey
16. Herschelle Gibbs and AB de Villiers
17. Eldine Baptiste
18. Jonathan Trott
19. Leicestershire
20. Fog

DIFFICULT

Quiz 80: Pot Luck

1. Which former England skipper has started a new career as a mixed martial artist?

2. Who was the only English-born batsman who batted in the 2010 T20 World Cup final?

3. Who were the four overseas-born batsmen who also batted for England in that 2010 T20 final?

4. Which country won the 2009 Women's World Cup?

5. Which American actor and comedian said, 'Cricket is basically baseball on valium'?

6. McLean Park is a Test match venue in which city?

7. Who was the only cricketer to be knighted while still playing the game?

8. Which three players captained England's Twenty20 team in 2011?

9. Who is the only Indian to have scored a Test century and double century in the same match?

10. Which West Indian is the only person to have scored five centuries in five Test innings?

11. In 1980, which Englishman became the first batsman to be dismissed for 99 in a One-Day International?

12. Who is the only England bowler since the war to be hit for over 200 runs in a single Test innings?

13. Who is the only captain to take nine wickets in a Test match innings?

14. Who was the first batsman to score 6,000 One-Day International runs?

15. Which Bangladeshi wicket-keeper didn't concede a single bye during Pakistan's 594 for 5 in 2011?

16. Who bowled 60 overs during England's Test defeat at the hands of South Africa in 2008 without taking a wicket?

17. Which Australian spinner went for 358 runs in a Test match against India in 2008?

18. Which Northamptonshire left-arm seam bowler made two Test appearances for England in the mid-1990s?

19. Who did Kevin Pietersen dismiss to claim his first Test wicket?
    a) Inzamam ul Haq
    b) Kamran Akmal
    c) Umar Gul

20. At which ground will you find a statue of a heckling spectator nicknamed Yabba?
    a) The Gabba
    b) The MCG
    c) The SCG

Answers to Quiz 79: All-Rounders

1. Rikki Clarke
2. Chennai Super Kings
3. Charles Burgess
4. Jacques Kallis
5. Josh Cobb
6. Dwayne Bravo
7. Mike Watkinson
8. Derek Pringle (his father was Don)
9. Ravi Bopara
10. Franklyn Stephenson
11. Durham
12. Ronnie Irani
13. Darren Sammy
14. Graham Gooch
15. Norman 'Mandy' Mitchell-Innes
16. Marlon Samuels
17. Mushtaq Mohammed
18. Alan Davidson
19. Jeff Wilson
20. Andrew Hall

DIFFICULT

Quiz 81: Fast Bowlers

1. Which quickie took his 50th wicket in just his seventh Test in 2012, becoming the fastest to a half-century of dismissals since Tom Richardson in 1893?

2. Who are the two fast-bowling captains to have taken 13 wickets in a Test match?

3. Which Indian seamer took 13 for 132 against Pakistan in 1999 but still ended up on the losing side?

4. Who is the only captain to take seven wickets in a One-Day International?

5. Which fast bowler has dismissed Sachin Tendulkar the most times in Test cricket?

6. Which legendary paceman bowled a 15-ball over in a Test match in Perth in 1996/97?

7. Montgomery Everton are the middle names of which legendary fast bowler?

8. Which Australian seamer collected his 300th first-class wicket on his side's 2012 tour of the West Indies?

9. Which mercurial fast bowler was named the 2009 ICC Cricketer of the Year?

10. Which former Australian fast bowler has the same name as one of the main characters in Brett Easton Ellis's novel American Psycho?

11. Who is the most prolific South African wicket-taker in Test matches against England?

12. Who are the two bowlers to have taken seven wickets in a One-Day International against England?

13. Which speedster has taken the most wickets against England in ODIs?

14. La Bertram is the middle name of which West Indies fast bowler?

15. Which left-arm quickie retired from the game after being called for throwing in a 1963 Test against South Africa?

16. Robin Smith fractured his cheekbone in a 1995 Test match after being hit by a delivery from which rapid West Indian?

17. Which Australian paceman was temporarily deported from the UK in May 2012 after a visa error?

18. Which West Indian fast bowler, who played only two Test matches, is best known for breaking Graham Gooch's finger in a 1990 Test in Trinidad?

19. Balfour is the real first name of which fearsome West Indian quickie?
    a) Michael Holding b) Patrick Patterson c) Courtney Walsh

20. Which of the following West Indian quicks took the most Test wickets? a) Joel Garner b) Michael Holding c) Andy Roberts

Answers to Quiz 80: Pot Luck

1. Adam Hollioake
2. Paul Collingwood
3. Richard Lumb, Craig Kieswetter, Kevin Pietersen and Eoin Morgan
4. England
5. Robin Williams
6. Napier
7. Sir Richard Hadlee
8. Paul Collingwood, Graeme Swann and Stuart Broad
9. Sunil Gavaskar
10. Everton Weekes
11. Geoff Boycott
12. Ian Botham (against Pakistan in 1987)
13. Kapil Dev
14. Viv Richards
15. Mushfiqur Rahim
16. Monty Panesar
17. Jason Krezja
18. Paul Taylor
19. Kamran Akmal
20. SCG

DIFFICULT

Quiz 82: Pot Luck

1. Which former Kent and Warwickshire spinner was romantically involved with the sister of the Duchess of Cambridge, Pippa Middleton?

2. Who smashed a century off just 45 balls for South Africa in a T20 international against New Zealand in 2012?

3. How many Test centuries did Brian Lara score at Lord's?

4. Who holds the record for being run out the most times in a Test match?

5. Don Bradman is one of only two men to be dismissed in a Test match for 299. Who, in 1991, became the second?

6. Who scored a century in both innings for England against India in 2008 but still ended up on the losing side?

7. Which West Indian is the only player to score five centuries in a single five Test series?

8. Who are the only two England batsmen with 2,000 Test runs against the West Indies?

9. Since the war, which batsman holds the record for the highest innings against Australia?

10. Who was the first Englishman to score 5,000 One-Day International runs?

11. Lancashire fielded two overseas players in the 2011 County Championship season, one Sri Lankan and one Pakistani. Who were they?

12. Which Glamorgan player holds the record for scoring the most first-class runs without playing a Test match?

13. Which English batsman scored a duck and a double hundred in his debut first-class match in 1996?

14. A cricket match from which novel by Charles Dickens appeared on a £10 note?

15. Woodbridge Road is an occasional venue for which English county?

16. Which South African's unbeaten 309 against Glamorgan in 2006 is Leicestershire's highest first-class innings?

17. The Walker Ground and Old Deer Park are venues used by which English county?

18. Which West Indian fast bowler hit 36 sixes in his Test career in a total of 910 runs?

19. Who holds the record for the fastest Test century by an opening batsman?
    a) Chris Gayle
    b) Gordon Greenidge
    c) David Warner

20. Who was the first President of the USA to attend a Test match?
    a) George W Bush
    b) Dwight Eisenhower
    c) Ronald Reagan

Answers to Quiz 81: Fast Bowlers

1. Vernon Philander
2. Courtney Walsh and Waqar Younis
3. Javagal Srinath
4. Waqar Younis
5. Brett Lee
6. Curtly Ambrose
7. Andy Roberts
8. Ben Hilfenhaus
9. Mitchell Johnson
10. Craig McDermott
11. Shaun Pollock
12. Waqar Younis and Andy Bichel
13. Brett Lee
14. Tino Best
15. Ian Meckiff
16. Ian Bishop
17. Mitchell Starc
18. Ezra Moseley
19. Patrick Patterson
20. Joel Garner

DIFFICULT

Quiz 83: Australia

1. Who are the four Australians to have their portrait hung in the Long Room at Lord's?

2. Who are the two Australians to have scored a Test match triple century and taken five wickets in a Test match innings?

3. Which English-born seam bowler took 6 for 39 in a 1983 Cricket World Cup match against India?

4. Who has scored Australia's highest One-Day International innings?

5. Who took 41 wickets in the 1978/79 Test series against England?

6. Which Australian scored the first run in Test cricket and the first Test century?

7. Since 2000, three Australian spinners have taken five wickets in each innings of a Test match. Shane Warne and Stuart MacGill are two. Who is the third?

8. Who holds the record for the most runs in the Cricket World Cup for Australia without scoring a century?

9. What is Australia's lowest score in a Test match innings?

10. Which batsman, who scored a century on his Test debut, managed just 17 runs at an average of 2.83, in the four Test series against India in 2011/12?

11. Who was the last Australian to score a century and take five wickets in the same Test match?

12. Which current Australian Test player played in England for the British Universities?

13. Who did John Inverarity succeed as the Australian chairman of selectors?

14. Who was the Man of the Match in the 1987 World Cup final?

15. Excluding England, Australia have been defeated the most times in Test matches by which opponents?

16. Who scored a century on his Test debut at the Oval in 1981?

17. What record was set during Australia's innings of 279 in the 2005 Ashes Test at Edgbaston?

18. Which Aussie scored a century in both innings in a 2009 Test match in Durban?

19. Who played a record-breaking 175 first-class matches before making his Test debut?
a) Brad Hodge
b) Michael Hussey
c) Andrew Symonds

20. Who has scored the most Test runs for Australia without ever reaching fifty?
a) Ray Bright
b) Craig McDermott
c) Jeff Thomson

Answers to Quiz 82: Pot Luck

1. Alex Loudon
2. Richard Levi
3. None
4. Ricky Ponting
5. Martin Crowe
6. Andrew Strauss
7. Clyde Walcott
8. Graham Gooch and Geoffrey Boycott
9. VVS Laxman with 291
10. Paul Collingwood
11. Farveez Maharoof and Junaid Khan
12. Alan Jones
13. David Sales
14. The Pickwick Papers
15. Surrey
16. Hylton Ackerman
17. Middlesex
18. Michael Holding
19. David Warner
20. Dwight Eisenhower

DIFFICULT

Quiz 84: Pot Luck

1. Who is the only player to score a century in a World Cup final and end up on the losing side?

2. The pavilion at the Windsor Park, in Dominica is named after which umpire?

3. Which Pakistani pair put on a record-breaking last wicket partnership of 151 against South Africa in 1997?

4. Who is the only Zimbabwean to have scored a century and taken five wickets in an innings in the same Test match?

5. Who are the three left-handed West Indian bowlers to have take 100 Test wickets?

6. The Most Promising Young Player at each county cricket team is given a medal named after what player?

7. Which former England bowler made two guest appearances in TV soap Family Affairs?

8. Which South African was named Player of the Tournament at the 1999 World Cup?

9. Which Indian was the leading scorer in One-Day Internationals in 2011?

10. Which artist painted The Cricket Match, which sold for £769,250 at auction in 2008?

11. The Redbacks is the nickname of which Australian state side?

12. Who scored half-centuries in the 1999, 2003 and 2007 World Cup finals?

13. Which team dismissed Somerset for just 50 in a County Championship game at Taunton in 2011?

14. Which England spinner lost four toes in an accident involving a speedboat propeller in 1968?

15. Who are the three Lancastrians since the war to have scored 7,000 runs and taken 700 first-class wickets?

16. Which Pakistani is the only bowler to take five wickets in an innings in three successive ODIs?

17. Which South African was dismissed first ball in his Test debut for South Africa against India in 1992?

18. Which seamer scored his maiden Test century in his 97th Test match?

19. Which of the following England spinners took the most Test wickets?
    a) Phil Edmonds
    b) Ray Illingworth
    c) Phil Tufnell

20. Both Andrew Flintoff and Steve Harmison ended their Test career having taken the same number of wickets. How many?
    a) 226
    b) 236
    c) 246

Answers to Quiz 83: Australia

1. Victor Trumper, Don Bradman, Keith Miller and Shane Warne
2. Bobby Simpson and Michael Clarke
3. Ken MacLeay
4. Shane Watson
5. Rodney Hogg
6. Charles Bannerman
7. Colin Miller
8. Michael Clarke
9. 36
10. Shaun Marsh
11. Richie Benaud
12. Ed Cowan
13. Andrew Hilditch
14. David Boon
15. West Indies
16. Dirk Wellham
17. It's Australia's highest Test score that didn't feature a batsman making a 50
18. Phil Hughes
19. Michael Hussey
20. Craig McDermott

DIFFICULT

Quiz 85: Taking the Michael

Can you identify the following cricketing Michaels?

1. Played 18 Tests for Australia between 1994 and 1998 but never reached three figures?

2. After retiring from the game took to painting using a technique called Artballing?

3. He has played county cricket for Sussex and Durham, ODIs for Australia and T2os for Italy?

4. All-rounder who could bowl medium pace or spin, played four Tests for England in the 1990s?

5. Australian left-arm quickie who made a cameo appearance on TV soap Neighbours?

6. Made 30 and 34 in his only Test innings to date in 2010?

7. Opened the batting for England in World Twenty20 final in 2010?

8. Holds the record for the highest score by a Sussex batsman against a touring team?

9. Left-handed batsman who played 20 Tests for Sri Lanka between 2001 and 2008?

10. Helped put on a record-breaking last-wicket partnership for the West Indies in a 1984 ODI against England?

11. This former England seamer has the middle names Walter William?

12. First Scotsman to captain the England Test team?

13. Played a single Test for England in 1997 but a famous dropped catch by Graham Thorpe meant he ended up wicketless?

14. Took 41 wickets at an average of just 15.02 in a curtailed Test career. Now an ICC Match Referee?

15. Opener who played 39 matches for England despite averaging less than 23 with the bat?

16. Seamer who took 87 wickets at under 26 in 30 Tests between 1974 and 1981 but never managed a five-wicket haul?

17. This former England opener later wrote a book called 'Gambling: A Story of Triumph and Disaster'?

18. Australian seamer who was smashed for 113 from 10 overs by South Africa's batsmen in a 2006 ODI?

19. The long-time groundsman at Lord's?

20. County coach whose name is the same as a film director and former Luton and Blackburn Rovers striker?

Answers to Quiz 84: Pot Luck

1. Mahela Jayawardene
2. Billy Doctrove
3. Azhar Mahmood and Mushtaq Ahmed
4. Paul Strang
5. Garfield Sobers, Alf Valentine and Pedro Collins
6. Denis Compton
7. Phil Tufnell
8. Lance Klusener
9. Virat Kohli
10. LS Lowry
11. South Australia
12. Adam Gilchrist
13. Warwickshire
14. Fred Titmus
15. Jack Simmons, Mike Watkinson and Glen Chapple
16. Waqar Younis
17. Jimmy Cook
18. Chaminda Vaas
19. Phil Edmonds
20. 226

DIFFICULT

175

Quiz 86: Pot Luck

1. Who are the five England batsmen to have scored Test match triple centuries?

2. Before Strauss and Cook, who were the last England openers to compile a double-century opening partnership?

3. Which England batsman scored a century on his ODI debut in 1972 and in his last ODI in 1977?

4. The son of which former England football manager was on the staff at Middlesex CCC in 2012?

5. Who is the only West Indian Test player whose Christian name begins with the letter X?

6. What was the name of the 1990s TV comedy starring Roger Daws, Brenda Blethyn and Timothy Spall?

7. Which country made its international tournament debut at the 2010 World Twenty20?

8. Which Englishman's 22-match Test career stretched from 1949 to 1976?

9. In which city will you find a Test match venue called Carisbrook?

10. Can you name the three bowlers that took seven wickets in an innings in the final Ashes Test at the Oval in 1997?

11. What is the name of the award given by the Cricket Society to the leading all-rounder in English first-class cricket?

12. Reg Foster is the only Englishman to have done what?

13. Which Australian holds the record for the highest first-class score by a Durham batsman?

14. Which pair, who started their partnership with the score at 92 for 9, put on 117 for England's last wicket against the West Indies at The Oval in 1980?

15. Which rugby league international played second XI cricket for Essex in the mid-1980s?

16. Which player has been on the losing side the most often in Test cricket history?

17. Which batsman reached 1,000 ODI runs in the shortest number of matches?

18. Which Aussie was on the winning side in his first 15 Test appearances?

19. Which county were dismissed for just 44 in the first innings of a 2010 County Championship game but still went on to win by 54 runs?
    a) Derbyshire
    b) Leicestershire
    c) Northamptonshire

20. Who was asked by David Cameron to stand as a Conservative candidate for the Barnsley Central by-election in 2011?
    a) Dickie Bird
    b) Geoffrey Boycott
    c) Darren Gough

Answers to Quiz 85: Taking the Michael

1. Michael Bevan
2. Michael Vaughan
3. Michael Di Venuto
4. Mike Watkinson
5. Mike Whitney
6. Michael Carberry
7. Michael Lumb
8. Michael Yardy
9. Michael Vandort
10. Michael Holding
11. Mike Selvey
12. Mike Denness
13. Mike Smith
14. Mike Procter
15. Mike Brearley
16. Mike Hendrick
17. Michael Atherton
18. Mick Lewis
19. Mick Hunt
20. Mike Newell

DIFFICULT

Quiz 87: England

1. Who holds the record for the most consecutive Test appearances for England?

2. Which England batsman scored a half-century in eight consecutive Test matches in 2004?

3. Name the six foreign-born players who played for England in the 1992 World Cup final?

4. And can you name the five English-born players?

5. Who has scored the most One-Day International runs for England without ever scoring a century?

6. Virgil is the nickname of which former England captain?

7. Only two England batsmen, both openers, have retired with a One-Day International average of over 40. Can you name them?

8. Which seam bowler was the first player to take 4 wickets in a Twenty20 game for England?

9. Who holds the record for the most wickets in a single Test series?

10. Which England player was formerly a chorister at St Paul's Cathedral School?

11. Who is the only England bowler to have taken at least 100 Test wickets to have a bowling average of over 40?

12. Which Durham player helped put on 100 for the ninth wicket with Vikram Solanki in a 2005 ODI against Pakistan?

13. How many different venues have hosted Test cricket in England?

14. Jonathan Trott dismissed which Pakistani batsman in a 2012 Test in Dubai?

15. Can you name the two England players to have been dismissed for a duck 13 times in One-Day International cricket?

16. Which pair enjoyed a record-breaking partnership of 411 in the 1957 Edgbaston Test against the West Indies?

17. Which wicket-keeper has recorded the most Test stumpings for England?

18. Who has the dubious honour of being hit for the most runs in a single Twenty20 international?

19. Which post-war bowler has taken 10 wickets in a Test match the most times?
    a) Ian Botham
    b) Fred Trueman
    c) Derek Underwood

20. Who has passed fifty the most times in Test cricket for England?
    a) Michael Atherton
    b) Geoffrey Boycott
    c) Graham Gooch

Answers to Quiz 86: Pot Luck

1. Andy Sandham, John Edrich, Graham Gooch, Wally Hammond and Len Hutton
2. Strauss and Trescothick
3. Dennis Amiss
4. Glen Hoddle (his son is Jamie)
5. Xavier Marshall
6. Outside Edge
7. Afghanistan
8. Brian Close
9. Dunedin
10. Glenn McGrath, Michael Kasprowicz and Phil Tufnell
11. The Wetherall Award
12. Captained the England football and cricket teams
13. Martin Love
14. Peter Willey and Bob Willis
15. Martin Offiah
16. Shivnarine Chanderpaul
17. Jonathan Trott
18. Adam Gilchrist
19. Derbyshire
20. Darren Gough

DIFFICULT

Quiz 88: Pot Luck

1. Which Pakistani spinner locked his wife in a cupboard the night before the 1999 World Cup final to avoid disciplinary action from officials who had banned family visits?

2. How many Test centuries has Ricky Ponting scored at Lord's?

3. Which South African pair put on a Test record of 415 for the opening wicket against Bangladesh in 2008?

4. What do Marvan Atapattu, Graham Gooch and Saeed Anwar have in common?

5. Which all-rounder took a wicket with his first ball in One-Day International cricket against Pakistan in 2003?

6. Which Egyptian-born spinner made his Test debut for South Africa in 1970, then played his second Test for Zimbabwe 23 years later?

7. Which English county ground has ends called the River End and the Hayes Close End?

8. Who, in 1976, became the youngest player to score a Test match double hundred?

9. Which West Indian scored a fifty in seven successive Test innings in 2006 and 2007?

10. Ropery Lane was a former ground of which county?

11. Cleophas is the middle name of which Ashes-winning bowler?

12. Which Yorkshireman was the oldest man to play Test cricket?

13. England's first total of 200 plus in a T20 international was a losing chase against which opposition in 2007?

14. Who has taken the most wickets for India in Test matches against England?

15. Who is the only batsman to have been dismissed in the 90s in both innings of two Test matches?

16. England's best ever Twenty20 partnership of 128 was set in 2011 against the West Indies by Craig Kieswetter and which other batsman?

17. Which nightwatchman opened the batting for Sri Lanka in the second Test against England in 2012?

18. Who holds the record for the most Test runs for the West Indies against England?

19. Which former England captain stood against future prime minister James Callaghan at the 1964 general election?
    a) Colin Cowdrey
    b) Ted Dexter
    c) Tony Lewis

20. Who is the only England player to have played in over 50 Test match defeats?
    a) Michael Atherton
    b) Ian Botham
    c) Alec Stewart

Answers to Quiz 87: England

1. Alastair Cook
2. Andrew Flintoff
3. Hick, Lamb, Lewis, Reeve, Pringle, DeFreitas
4. Gooch, Botham, Stewart, Fairbrother, Illingworth
5. Graham Thorpe
6. Michael Vaughan
7. Nick Knight and Chris Broad
8. Jon Lewis
9. SF Barnes with 49

10. Alastair Cook
11. Ashley Giles at 40.60
12. Liam Plunkett
13. 10
14. Younis Khan
15. Alec Stewart and Marcus Trescothick
16. Peter May and Colin Cowdrey
17. Godfrey Evans
18. James Anderson
19. Derek Underwood
20. Graham Gooch

DIFFICULT

Quiz 89: County Cricket

1. Which Kent batsman-turned-umpire is the only man to score two double centuries in the same first-class match?

2. Which all-rounder scored two centuries and took 11 wickets in a 1988 Championship match for Nottinghamshire and still ended up on the losing side?

3. Who are the three batsmen to have scored a century against all 18 first-class counties?

4. Which Lancashire batsman hit 34 from an over in a 1977 game against Glamorgan?

5. Mark Ramprakash was one of two players to score a double century and a century in the 2010 County Championship. Which Australian was the other?

6. Who scored a century in both innings of Sussex's 2011 County Championship match against Yorkshire?

7. Which member of a famous cricketing family took 4 wickets in 4 balls in Surrey's 2000 Championship match against Derbyshire?

8. Which 42-year-old, in 1961, became the last man to score 3,000 runs in an English first-class summer?

9. Which bowler took his 500th first-class wicket in the 2012 County Championship match between Glamorgan and Essex?

10. Which South African-born batsman was the leading first-class run-scorer in England in 2008?

11. Who holds the record for the most runs in a first-class match in a single day?

12. Which West Indian scored 1,186 runs and took 56 wickets in the 1996 County Championship?

13. Which batsman reached 1,000 runs in a season in 28 consecutive seasons between 1907 and 1938?

14. Since the number of County Championship matches was reduced in 1969, who is the only man to have scored 2,000 runs in a season five times?

15. Which former Derbyshire all-rounder was the last man to

score a century and take 10 wickets in the same County Championship match?

16. Who were the sponsors of the County Championship from 1984 until 1998?

17. Who holds the record for the most centuries in a County Championship season?

18. The lowest ever score in a County Championship match was recorded by which county?
    a) Derbyshire
    b) Leicestershire
    c) Northamptonshire

19. In what year did Glamorgan win their first County Championship?
    a) 1938
    b) 1948
    c) 1958

Answers to Quiz 88: Pot Luck

1. Saqlain Mushtaq
2. None
3. Graeme Smith and Neil McKenzie
4. They all made a pair on their Test debut
5. Rikki Clarke
6. John Traicos
7. Chelmsford's County Ground
8. Javed Miandad
9. Shivnarine Chanderpaul
10. Durham
11. Gladstone Small
12. Wilfred Rhodes
13. India
14. Bhagwath Chandrasekhar with 95
15. Gordon Greenidge
16. Alex Hales
17. Dhammika Prasad
18. Garfield Sobers
19. Ted Dexter
20. Alec Stewart

DIFFICULT

Quiz 90: Pot Luck

1. Who is the only player to appear on the Lord's Honours Board as both a home player and as a visitor?

2. Which pair are the most prolific partnership in Test cricket?

3. Which West Indian scored a century in his ODI debut in 1978 and in his last ODI in 1994?

4. Who was the first Bangladeshi to score a century and take five wickets in an innings in the same Test match?

5. Which Zimbabwean bowler turned commentator had a Test match batting average of just 2 in his 15 Test career?

6. Cazaly's Stadium is a Test venue in which city?

7. How many Test match appearances did Graham Thorpe make?

8. Which Indian hit six fours from a Bob Willis over at Old Trafford in 1982?

9. As well as playing cricket for South Africa, Jonty Rhodes also represented his country in what other sport?

10. Which all-rounder scored a half century in just 24 balls in a 2005 Test match against Zimbabwe?

11. Which England seam bowler has a daughter called Indiana and a son called Darley?

12. Who holds the record for the highest ODI score for Ireland?

13. Which Zimbabwean scored a then-record ODI innings of 194 not out against Bangladesh but still ended up on the losing side?

14. Who won the World Cup as a player in 1987 and as a coach in 1999?

15. Which batsman faced the first ball in ODI history?

16. Which Australian has scored the most runs in a first-class season for Durham?

17. Who took 5 for 36, including a hat trick, in an ODI against Pakistan in 1997 but never played for Australia again?

18. Which Hollywood A-lister is a cousin of a prolific New Zealand batsman?

19. England compiled their lowest ever ODI score in a game in 2001. How many did they make?
    a) 85
    b) 86
    c) 87

20. Who were their opponents in that game?
    a) Australia
    b) Pakistan
    c) Sri Lanka

Answers to Quiz 89: County Cricket

1. Arthur Fagg in 1938
2. Franklyn Stephenson
3. Carl Hooper, Mark Ramprakash and Chris Adams
4. Frank Hayes
5. Chris Rogers
6. Michael Yardy
7. Gary Butcher
8. Bill Alley
9. Dean Cosker
10. Stephen Moore
11. Brian Lara
12. Phil Simmons
13. Frank Woolley
14. Graham Gooch
15. Graham Wagg
16. Britannic Assurance
17. Wally Hammond
18. Northamptonshire
19. 1948

DIFFICULT

Quiz 91: Spinners part 2

1. Which spinner's career spanned five decades, from 1949 until 1982?

2. Who is the only Australian to play Test cricket since the war whose first name begins with the letter X?

3. Which England spinner was sick on the pitch during a 1996 World Cup game?

4. Who took 6 wickets and scored 37 runs on his Test debut in 2010 and hasn't played a Test since?

5. Which spinner, who made his ODI debut in 2012, is the first England international to be born on the Isle of Wight?

6. David Kenneth are the middle names of which former England spinner?

7. Who took nine wickets and scored a century batting at 8 in India's 2011 drawn Test with the West Indies?

8. Which spinner has played in Tests and T20 games for England but never appeared in a One-Day International?

9. Who was leading wicket-taker in English county cricket in 2009?

10. Since 1970, only two England left-arm spinners have taken 5 wickets in both innings of the same Test match. Derek Underwood is one. Can you name the other?

11. Which 44-year-old spinner captained England on his ODI debut in 1985?

12. Prior to Ian Salisbury, who was the last specialist leg-spinner to play for England?

13. In terms of wickets taken, who is the most successful Australian spinner in the Cricket World Cup?

14. Candles is the nickname of which former Australian spinner?

15. Who is the only player to take 300 wickets in an English first-class season?

16. Which 36-year-old spinner made his Test debut against the West Indies in 1988?

17. Graeme Swann took two wickets in his first over in Test cricket. Rahul Dravid was one, who was the other?

18. Who took 5 for 86 to steer Australia to victory in the third Test against the West Indies in Dominica in 2012?

19. Who was the first Indian to take a Test match hat trick?
    a) Bishan Bedi
    b) Harbhajan Singh
    c) Anil Kumble

20. Who was the first bowler to take 600 Test wickets?
    a) Anil Kumble
    b) Muttiah Muralitharan
    c) Shane Warne

Answers to Quiz 90: Pot Luck

1. Gordon Greenidge (He scored a century for MCC v Rest of the World and for West Indies against England)
2. Dravid and Tendulkar
3. Desmond Haynes
4. Shakib Al Hasan
5. Pommie Mbangwa
6. Cairns
7. 100
8. Sandeep Patil
9. Hockey
10. Jacques Kallis
11. Ryan Sidebottom
12. Paul Stirling
13. Charles Coventry
14. Geoff Marsh
15. Geoffrey Boycott
16. Michael Di Venuto
17. Anthony Stuart
18. Russell Crowe
19. 86
20. Australia

DIFFICULT

Quiz 92: Pot Luck

1. Which England captain scored just a single century in his 88 ODI matches?

2. Which famous fictional character was named after a Warwickshire all-rounder who was later killed in the First World War?

3. Who is the only player to play Test cricket for Australia whose surname starts with the letter Z?

4. What is the Dav of Dav Whatmore short for?

5. Which Yorkshire bowler holds the record for taking the most wickets in English cricket history?

6. Brian Lara joined Warwickshire in 1994 after injury ruled out which Indian all-rounder from becoming the county's overseas player that year?

7. Which Leicestershire all-rounder was a member of England's 1999 World Cup squad?

8. What middle name is shared by former England internationals David Lawrence and Matthew Fleming?

9. Which Indian is the only visiting player to score three Test match centuries at Lord's?

10. What name connects an Australian international captain and a famous movie character played by James Stewart?

11. England were dismissed for 88, their lowest total to date, in a 2011 T20 international. Who were their opponents?

12. Which former Lancashire all-rounder was appointed to the first-class umpiring list in 2011?

13. Which Sri Lankan opening batsman bagged a pair in two of his first three Test appearances?

14. England's biggest ODI victory was a 202-run thrashing of which Test-playing country?

15. Moggie is the nickname of which England international?

16. Who was the only batsman to score two centuries in the 2005 Ashes series?

17. Which left-arm seamer was the leading first-class wicket-taker in England in 1999?

18. Who has taken the most Test wickets for Pakistan in Test matches against England?

19. What was the margin of victory in the first ever T20 international between England and Australia?
    a) England won by 1 run
    b) England won by 10 runs
    c) England won by 100 runs

20. How many players were given a Test debut by England in 2011?
    a) none
    b) one
    c) two

Answers to Quiz 91: Spinners part 2

1. Fred Titmus
2. Xavier Doherty
3. Neil Smith
4. James Tredwell
5. Danny Briggs
6. Ian Salisbury
7. Ravichandran Ashwin
8. Chris Schofield
9. Danish Kaneria
10. Nick Cook
11. Norman Gifford
12. Robin Hobbs
13. Brad Hogg
14. Ray Bright
15. Alfred 'Tich' Freeman
16. John Childs
17. Gautham Gambhir
18. Michael Clarke
19. Harbhajan Singh
20. Shane Warne

DIFFICULT

Quiz 93: Batsmen

1. Which Aussie legend took 41 innings to record his first Test century?

2. Alastair Cook made a century on his Test debut in 2006 against which country?

3. Which batsman, who top-scored for England in the 1987 World Cup final, made his only Test century against Pakistan earlier that year?

4. Who was the second West Indian batsman to score 10,000 Test runs?

5. Which England batsman reached three figures in a Test match for the only time in his career against Pakistan at Headingley in 1996?

6. At 6ft 10in, who is the tallest player in the County Championship?

7. David Boon played for which Australian state side?

8. Which former England international is mentioned in the Manic Street Preachers song Mr Carbohydrate?

9. Which current Australian batsman studied to be a science teacher before starting his first-class career?

10. Who holds the record for recording the highest Test score yet still ending up on the losing side?

11. Which Sri Lankan has scored the most runs in the Cricket World Cup without making a century?

12. Which Aussie batsman had a highest Test score of 199 but a One-Day International best of just 1?

13. Who was the leading Test match run-scorer of the 1990s?

14. Which Australian scored the one millionth Test match run?

15. Who made an unbeaten 54 in his only Test appearance for Australia in 1995?

16. Who are the three players to have made a triple century and a double century in the same Test series?

17. Who was the first batsman to score 10,000 Test runs?

18. Which pair put on a record-breaking 470-run partnership for Warwickshire against Lancashire in 1982 but still lost the match by 10 wickets?

19. Who scored 84 runs in his only ODI appearance for England?
    a) Kim Barnett
    b) Monte Lynch
    c) Alan Wells

20. Actor and comedian Miles Jupp chose which England opening batsman as his chosen specialist subject on Celebrity Mastermind?
    a) Michael Atherton
    b) Geoffrey Boycott
    c) Andrew Strauss

Answers to Quiz 92: Pot Luck

1. Nasser Hussain
2. Jeeves
3. Tim Zoehrer
4. Davenell
5. Wilfred Rhodes
6. Manoj Prabhakar
7. Vince Wells
8. Valentine
9. Dilip Vengsarkar
10. George Bailey
11. West Indies
12. Steve O'Shaughnessy
13. Marvan Atapattu
14. India
15. Eoin Morgan
16. Andrew Strauss
17. Alamgir Sheriyar
18. Abdul Qadir
19. England won by 100 runs
20. None

DIFFICULT

Quiz 94: Pot Luck

1. Which city hosted the final of the 2009 Indian Premier League?

2. How many times were England bowled out in a Test match in 2011?

3. Which Surrey spinner took seven wickets in 11 balls in a 1972 County Championship match?

4. Who captained the England side that won the 1998 Under-19 Cricket World Cup?

5. Which former England batsman is now an agent with International Sports Management whose clients include Andrew Flintoff, Michael Vaughan and Ajmal Shahzad?

6. Who holds the record for the most runs in ODI cricket without scoring a century?

7. Which two non-English batsmen scored T20 centuries in the same innings for Gloucestershire against Middlesex in 2011?

8. Who were the three bowlers that took over 20 wickets in the 2005 Ashes series?

9. Which prolific West Indian batsman became an international bridge player after retiring from cricket?

10. The Iqbal Stadium is in which city?

11. Who are the two countries to have been bowled out twice in the same day in a Test match?

12. Who scored his only Test century for England against New Zealand in 2008?

13. At which English county ground will you find the Lynn Wilson Centre End?

14. Which cricketer was voted into office in the 2010 Sri Lankan general election?

15. Who averaged over 40 with the bat and 14 with the ball in four Tests for England in 2003 but never played another Test?

16. Which batsman has been out-stumped the most times in the history of Test cricket?

17. Who are the four West Indians to have scored 2,000 runs and taken 100 wickets in ODI cricket?

18. Who is the only batsman to score more than 150 in both innings of a Test match?

19. What is the Australian equivalent of the Barmy Army?
    a) The Cricket Tragics
    b) The Fanatics
    c) The Green and Gold Army

20. What is umpire Billy Bowden's real first name?
    a) Barnaby
    b) Bruce
    c) Brent

Answers to Quiz 93: Batsmen

1. Steve Waugh
2. India
3. Bill Athey
4. Shivnarine Chanderpaul
5. Nick Knight
6. Will Jefferson
7. Tasmania
8. Matthew Maynard
9. Michael Hussey
10. Ricky Ponting with 242 against India in 2003
11. Arjuna Ranatunga
12. Matthew Elliott
13. Alec Stewart
14. Allan Border
15. Stuart Law
16. Don Bradman, Wally Hammond and Michael Clarke
17. Sunil Gavaskar
18. Alvin Kallicharran and Geoff Humpage
19. Kim Barnett
20. Michael Atherton

DIFFICULT

Quiz 95: Swingers and Seamers

1. Which England bowler took 1,061 first-class wickets in a career that stretched from 1986 to 2006?

2. Which swing bowler made the last of his three Test appearances for England in an Ashes Test at Perth in 1991?

3. Which Australian seamer took a hat trick on his Test debut against Pakistan in 1994?

4. Which seamer, who played three Tests for England in the early 1990s, has the same name as a Wrexham and Swansea City striker?

5. Rupert is the middle name of which Aussie seamer who took 94 Test wickets between 2006 and 2009?

6. Who is the only man to take three wickets in a World Cup final for England?

7. Which Pakistani left-arm seamer took 5 for 63 on his Test debut against England at the Oval in 2010?

8. Which left-arm seamer won his one and only Test cap for England against Pakistan in 1996?

9. Which seamer, who played two Tests for England in the 1990s, took 737 first-class wickets for Warwickshire and Derbyshire?

10. Which England seamer once attended a Christmas fancy dress party as Diana Ross?

11. Who took 58 Test wickets for England in 1998?

12. Which Australian swinger took more Test wickets against England in England, 83, than he did against all opponents in Australia?

13. Which former Warwickshire and Worcestershire seamer has the same name as a former captain of Tottenham Hotspur?

14. Basil D'Oliveira was called up to England's 1968/69 Test squad to South Africa after an injury to which bowling all-rounder?

15. Which former miner made two Test appearances in the 1985 Ashes series?

16. Who took 1 for 122 on his only Test appearance for England against the West Indies in Trinidad in 2009?

17. Which Zambian-born seamer played three Tests and six ODIs for England between 1986 and 1988?

18. Which Aussie medium pacer took five wickets in his first 21 balls in the first Test against South Africa in 2011?

19. James Anderson took 5 for 73 on his Test debut at Lord's against which country?
    a) India
    b) New Zealand
    c) Zimbabwe

20. In 2003, Wasim Akram had a short spell with which English county?
    a) Hampshire
    b) Surrey
    c) Warwickshire

Answers to Quiz 94: Pot Luck

1. Johannesburg
2. Twice
3. Pat Pocock
4. Owais Shah
5. Neil Fairbrother
6. Wasim Akram
7. Kevin O'Brien and Hamish Marshall
8. Shane Warne, Andrew Flintoff and Brett Lee
9. Everton Weekes
10. Faisalabad
11. India and Zimbabwe
12. Tim Ambrose
13. The County Ground, Northampton
14. Sanath Jayasuriya
15. Anthony McGrath
16. Allan Border
17. Viv Richards, Chris Gayle, Carl Hooper and Dwayne Bravo
18. Allan Border
19. The Fanatics
20. Brent

DIFFICULT

Quiz 96: Pot Luck

1. Which cricket-obsessed stand-up comedian masqueraded as a journalist on England's 2006 tour of India and turned it into a stand-up show called Fibber in the Heat?

2. Bloomfield, Nondescripts and Moors are cricket clubs in which Asian city?

3. Who is the only England international whose surname contains the same letter four times?

4. In what country was Sussex all-rounder Ollie Rayner born?

5. Which England batsman scored 8,463 Test runs but never made a double century?

6. Who are the two players to have played ODIs for Australia whose surname starts with the letter V?

7. Who scored his one and only Test century for England in a match against India in Chennai in 1993?

8. Who is the oldest batsman to score an ODI century for England?

9. Which current first-class umpire took a wicket with the first ball in his first Test match in England in 2004?

10. Le Donk is the nickname of which all-rounder who has played one Test and 34 ODIs for England?

11. Which West Indies batsman died in a car crash in March 2012?

12. Which cricketer was the best man at Kevin Pietersen's wedding?

13. Can you name three Irish-born cricketers who have played for England since the 1990s?

14. Which former England batsman was given his middle name in honour of an England bowler killed in World War II?

15. Which West Indian-born bowler played his one and only Test for England at the age of 33 against South Africa in 1994?

16. Who was the first cricketer to appear on TV talent show Dancing On Ice?

17. Which batsman holds the record for the most international runs (Tests, ODIs and T20s) in a single year?

18. Who topped the bowling averages for England in the 2010/11 Ashes series?

19. Which Pakistani was the youngest to take five wickets in an innings in an ODI?
    a) Aqib Javed
    b) Waqar Younis
    c) Wasim Akram

20. What is the fewest number of runs scored in an uninterrupted day's play of Test cricket?
    a) 85
    b) 95
    c) 105

Answers to Quiz 95: Swingers and Seamers

1.	Martin Bicknell	11.	Angus Fraser
2.	Phil Newport	12.	Terry Alderman
3.	Damien Fleming	13.	Steve Perryman
4.	Steve Watkin	14.	Tom Cartwright
5.	Stuart Clark	15.	Les Taylor
6.	Derek Pringle	16.	Amjad Khan
7.	Wahab Riaz	17.	Neal Radford
8.	Simon Brown	18.	Shane Watson
9.	Tim Munton	19.	Zimbabwe
10.	Philip DeFreitas	20.	Hampshire

DIFFICULT

Quiz 97: Books

1. Which spinner's autobiography was called The Breaks are Off?

2. Coming Back to Me was an award winning book by which opening batsman?

3. Who was the first player to appear on the front cover of Wisden?

4. Which wicket-keeper wrote Keeping Quiet?

5. We'll Get 'Em In Sequins is a study of the changing face of manliness as told via cricketers from which county?

6. Which actor wrote The Last Flannelled Fool: My small part in English cricket's demise and its large part in mine?

7. Complete the title of Harry Pearson's book about Northern cricket: Slipless in...?

8. Behind The Shades was by which player turned coach?

9. Fox On The Run was an award winning diary by which former England opener?

10. The Big Ship by Gideon Haigh was a biography of which Australian captain?

11. Which quick bowler wrote the 2011 memoir Controversially Yours?

12. Duncan Hamilton won the William Hill Sports Book of the Year award in 2009 for his biography of which cricketer?

13. Line and Strength was the title of which metronomic bowler's autobiography?

14. Which former England batsman wrote the 2012 book Luck: What it Means and Why it Matters?

15. Sometimes I Forgot To Laugh was by which recently departed player turned journalist?

Answers – page 201

16. Which South African batsman's 2010 memoir was entitled To The Point?

17. Blood, Sweat And Treason is the autobiography of which fast bowler?

18. David Foot's Tormented Genius of Cricket was about which quick scoring Somerset batsman?

19. Which former Prime Minister wrote More Than A Game: The Story of Cricket's Early Years?
    a) Alec Douglas-Home
    b) John Howard
    c) John Major

20. What was the title of Harry Thompson's bestseller?
    a) Ducks Stopped Play
    b) Penguins Stopped Play
    c) Tigers Stopped Play

Answers to Quiz 96: Pot Luck

1. Miles Jupp
2. Colombo
3. Alan Mullally
4. Germany
5. Alec Stewart
6. Mike Veletta and Adam Voges
7. Chris Lewis
8. Geoffrey Boycott
9. Martin Saggers
10. Ian Blackwell
11. Runako Morton
12. Darren Gough
13. Ed Joyce, Eoin Morgan and Martin McCague
14. Nick Verity Knight (named after Hedley Verity)
15. Joey Benjamin
16. Dominic Cork
17. Ricky Ponting
18. Kevin Pietersen, whose one wicket cost 16 runs
19. Waqar Younis
20. 95

DIFFICULT

Quiz 98: Pot Luck

1. In which city will you find a Test match venue called Seddon Park?

2. Which left-arm New Zealand seamer took a Test hat trick against Bangladesh in 2004?

3. In which city will you find the Asgiriya Stadium?

4. Which former England batsman scored his 16,000th first-class run in April 2012?

5. Who took 6 for 77 for England in the second innings of England's 3-run win over Australia at Melbourne in 1982?

6. Which Kenyan faced just three balls at the 2011 World Cup and was dismissed every time?

7. Which English county has played home games at Archdeacon Meadow?

8. Who is the oldest post-war England batsman to make a maiden Test century?

9. Which left-handed batsman reached 8,000 Test runs in the fewest number of innings?

10. Which first-class fixture took place for the last time in Blackpool in September 1961?

11. Matt Prior is married to the daughter of which famous 'mooning' footballer?

12. Who was England's wicket-keeper for all five Tests in the 1994/95 Ashes series Down Under?

13. The legendary batsman George Headley was born in which Central American country?

14. According to Steve Marsh's autobiography, which former England bowler downed 72 pints of Guinness during his stag weekend in Dublin?

15. Which 7ft seamer played two ODIs for Pakistan against England in 2010?

16. Who was the first cricketer to appear on the front cover of gay lifestyle magazine Attitude?

17. Who is the oldest player to score a century in a One-Day International?

18. Who has faced the most balls in the history of Test cricket?

19. With one wicket for 9 runs, which batsman topped the bowling averages in the 2005 Ashes series?
    a) Simon Katich
    b) Ricky Ponting
    c) Michael Vaughan

20. South Africa dismissed Australia for what score in the 2011 Cape Town Test?
    a) 45
    b) 46
    c) 47

Answers to Quiz 97: Books

1. Graeme Swann	11. Shoaib Akhtar
2. Marcus Trescothick	12. Harold Larwood
3. Michael Vaughan	13. Glenn McGrath
4. Paul Nixon	14. Ed Smith
5. Yorkshire	15. Peter Roebuck
6. Michael Simkins	16. Herschelle Gibbs
7. Settle	17. Henry Olonga
8. Duncan Fletcher	18. Harold Gimblett
9. Graeme Fowler	19. John Major
10. Warwick Armstrong	20. Penguins Stopped Play

DIFFICULT

Quiz 99: Women's Cricket

1. True or false – the first Women's World Cup took place before the first men's World Cup?

2. Which two countries have played women's Test matches that aren't male Test-playing nations?

3. In what decade did the first women's Test match take place?

4. How many times have England won the Women's World Cup?

5. Who captained England to victory in the 2009 final?

6. Which England batsman was named Player of the Tournament after scoring 324 runs?

7. How many teams took part in the 2009 World Cup?

8. Who did England beat in the 2009 final?

9. Stefanie Taylor, who topped the ICC World Batting rankings in 2012 plays for which international side?

10. Who made her debut in the Test Match Special commentary box at the 2007 World Twenty20?

11. Which country will host the 2012 Women's World Twenty20?

12. Which country has won the Women's World Cup the most times?

13. Who made her England debut in 2005 at the age of just 15 years and 336 days?

14. Which teams compete for the Rose Bowl?

15. Who were the winners of the inaugural Women's World Twenty20?

16. What was the venue of that final?

17. Which Australian scored the first double century in a women's ODI before becoming the manager of the Australian Cricket Academy?

18. Shandre Fritz plays international cricket for which country?

19. In what year did the MCC accept female members for the first time?
    a) 1997
    b) 1998
    c) 1999

20. Which country will host the 2013 Wormen's World Cup?
    a) Australia
    b) India
    c) New Zealand

Answers to Quiz 98: Pot Luck

1. Hamilton
2. James Franklin
3. Kandy, Sri Lanka
4. Rob Key
5. Norman Cowans
6. Shem Ngoche
7. Gloucestershire
8. Basil D'Oliveira
9. Kumar Sangakkara
10. North versus South
11. Sammy Nelson
12. Steve Rhodes
13. Panama
14. Martin McCague
15. Mohammad Irfan
16. James Anderson
17. Sanath Jayasuriya
18. Rahul Dravid
19. Ricky Ponting
20. 47

DIFFICULT

Quiz 100: Pot Luck

1. Three Australians whose surname begins with I have won Test caps for Australia since the war. Can you name them?
2. Who was the last person to captain England on their Test debut?
3. Luteru is the real first name of which current New Zealand international?
4. Who are the two Pakistanis to have scored over 5,000 ODI runs and taken over 200 ODI wickets?
5. Which New Zealander once spent 77 balls and 101 minutes compiling a Test innings of 0 not out?
6. Which batsman's only Test century for Australia was an innings of 203 not out against South Africa at Perth in 2005?
7. Which county sometimes plays home games at the Chester Road North Ground?
8. What is the name of Basil D'Oliveira's brother, who played first-class cricket for Leicestershire?
9. Which Kenyan-born player was in England's 2007 World Cup squad?
10. Sexual Chocolate is the nickname of which former England international?
11. Which former England one-day player is the founder of a sports psychology consultancy called Sporting Edge?
12. Which current England international lists Watford striker Tommy Mooney as his sporting hero?
13. Who is the only Cornish-born player to play Test cricket for England since the war?
14. Which England bowler took two wickets in his first over in international cricket in a 2010 Twenty20 game against Pakistan?
15. Who, in 2010, became only the second player of Aboriginal origin to play international cricket for Australia?
16. Which England cricketer chose the first two series of TV comedy Friends as his chosen specialised subject on Celebrity Mastermind?

17. Which West Indian, who had spells with Sussex, Nottinghamshire, Warwickshire and Leicestershire, is one of just four players to have been timed out in first-class cricket?

18. Ricky Ponting was given 500 shares in which English football club in honour of his fundraising efforts for the club?

19. Who scored the most ODI runs out of
    a) Graeme Hick
    b) Allan Lamb
    c) Robin Smith

20. What is the most overs a bowler has sent down in a single test match innings?
    a) 78
    b) 88
    c) 98

Answers to Quiz 99: Women's Cricket

1. True
2. Ireland and the Netherlands
3. 1930s
4. Three times
5. Charlotte Edwards
6. Claire Taylor
7. Eight
8. New Zealand
9. West Indies
10. Alison Mitchell
11. Sri Lanka
12. Australia
13. Holly Colvin
14. Australia and New Zealand
15. England
16. Lord's
17. Belinda Clark
18. South Africa
19. 1999
20. India

DIFFICULT

Keeping Score

Keeping Score

Keeping Score

Keeping Score

Keeping Score

Keeping Score

Keeping Score

Keeping Score

Keeping Score

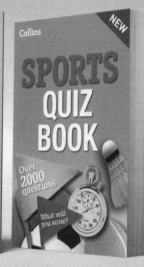